Development
of the
Creative Individual

Development of the Creative Individual

John Curtis Gowan

San Fernando Valley State College
Northridge, California

Robert R. Knapp, *Publisher*
San Diego, California 92107

FIRST EDITION

LIBRARY OF CONGRESS NUMBER 73-179138

ISBN 0-912736-11-9

MANUFACTURED IN THE UNITED STATES OF AMERICA

SAN DIEGO, CALIFORNIA 92107

Contents

Chapter   **Page**

List of Illustrations

Preface

This is a book of glimpses; glimpses of theory, glimpses of practice and glimpses of a better future. These glimpses are doubtless distorted by the writer's bias and idiosyncrasy; but time will cure this, for someday a younger and abler writer will write a clearer and better book. Such is the way of progress. Meanwhile, the glimpses will provide some with hope and others with the material for derision. For it is a principle which the book enunciates—that those higher abilities which man will someday hold securely appear to him today in tenuous fits and starts.

Since truth asks for no more than coexistence, hypotheses, like people, are best judged by their consequential behavior and not by their pedigree. The reader must expect to be subjected to the views of original but out-of-fashion writers such as Bucke and Sheldon. In this regard, the testimony of a man of Maslow's (1959, p. 89) genius is noteworthy:

> It was a startling thing for me to hear a woman describing her feelings as she gave birth to a child in the same words used by Bucke (1929) to describe the "cosmic consciousness." . . . I had to respect constitutional difference of the Sheldonian sort more than I had, as Morris (1956) had also discovered.

Theories that make any kind of sense out of experience, whether they are visionary like Bucke's or statistically suspect like Sheldon's, deserve respect not on the basis of pedigree but on how much experience they bind and how much sense they make. The connecting of experience in any form is too valuable an act to go unrecognized, whether or not it agrees with other modes or fashions of experiential conceptualization. History is full of circumstances where a theory neglected for years suddenly is redeemed through the discovery of some new facts. We do not have time in the future for this kind of luxury lag in hypotheses formulation.

The theme of this volume is: "What accounts for the creative development of superior individuals?" The author has been preoccupied with this question for a number of years having first considered it in a volume by Gowan and Demos (1964) and again the next year in "What Makes A Gifted Child Creative?" (Gowan, 1965). But the answers seemed too glib and too superficial, despite another attempt in 1967 (Gowan, Demos and Torrance, 1967). The outcome of several years' study and attention to this matter is the present volume, which mounts a much more detailed investigation into the process.

The plan of this volume is to scrutinize the process of individual development, with special attention to the development of the superior individual, and to attempt to justify the inclusion of creative production as a process in that developmental escalation. This developmental direction, as Piaget noted, is away from the egocentric toward greater freedom and self-actualization.

This plan is carried out in seven chapters.[1] The first, an introductory chapter, makes a selective search of the literature in regard to development and creativity. In chapter 2 the existence and periodicity of eight developmental stages is enunciated. Chapter 3 devotes itself to the important concept of escalation with its five attributes of succession, discontinuity, emergence, differentiation and integration. Chapter 4 discusses creativity, and particularly its preconscious sources in relation to developmental stages. Chapter 5 is concerned with the environmental stimulation necessary for creativity at every level. Chapter 6 discusses the problems and penalties of remaining noncreative. Chapter 7 is devoted to the process of self-actualization as it relates to the last three adult cognitive stages of creativity, psychedelia and illumination.

This book will please neither those who advocate nor those who oppose the use of drugs to gain psychedelic effects—an area not of the writer's competency—thus it has been neglected purposely. This action will not please those who aver that the use of drugs is a short cut to Nirvana. Conversely, despite urging by well-meaning individuals to denounce the use of drugs, this too has been avoided for it seems as blameworthy to denounce a method out of prejudice as to advocate it out of ignorance. There are psychedelic effects which are related to both creativity and personal development and these are possible without the involvement of drugs.

Some readers may be surprised by the extensive use that has been made of analogs from physical science. It seems that the tradition started by Lewin is well worth continuing, both because the images of physical science are so clear and discrete and because it is so much better organized at the present time than behavioral science. Modeling from the physical sciences to the behavioral sciences is one way of "piggy-backing" on the extensive accomplishments of physical science in an effort to catch up.

Another feature of the book which will appeal to some readers and not to others is the extensive use of poetry. This action has been rather in the nature of a "happening" than by deliberate design. The poet, however, often is a prophet, and it is he who first foresees the onward course of progress so that, very often, new innovations are first announced implicitly in poetry long before they are adduced by psychological investigation. In several places in the book, poetry has proved to be a happy and appropriate explication of an idea being developed.

Some well-meaning individuals, after reading parts of the manuscript, have

---

[1]The lay reader who is uninterested in the literature of development and creativity may wish to skip chapter 1. Some readers may also find Chapter 3 difficult.

said in effect that the book is on religion and that a new type of religious practice is advocated. The charge I wish strongly to refute. The author, a psychologist, not a theologian, is not religiously oriented and is not a member of any organized sect. It appears that religion may have been confused with value. The attempt has been made in these pages to show that the process of development has values and that these values come out of psychologic analysis of man. (This is because they are inherent in man.) Since values have commonly been ascribed to religion in the past, many people think that that is where the values belong; but the history of culture shows first physical science and now behavioral science constantly taking over realms once considered the preserve of religion. The "Krathwohl-Bloom Taxonomy of Educational Objectives in the Affective Domain" is an excellent example of psychologically oriented values. It is felt that those presented in this volume are similar.

Acknowledgments

No person could write a book of this type without being obligated to many other minds, some contemporary, but most in the past. All explorers must stand on the shoulders of those who have gone before. This is especially true when theories are to be modified or extended. An attempt has been made to give suitable acknowledgment wherever this has happened, but a general acknowledgment is also appropriate here. To such men as Freud, Erikson, Sullivan, Kubie, Piaget, Bruner, and Guilford I am greatly indebted, and it should be understood that this author assumes responsibility whenever extension of their theories has been suggested.

I wish to acknowledge the courtesy of many authors, copyright holders and publishers for permission to use selections of their works to illustrate points. Similarly acknowledgment is made of the courtesy of copyright holders of my own previous works, such as Ann Isaacs, C. C. Thomas, David McKay, and John Wiley & Sons, for permission to use, abridge, expand, modify and develop material and themes initially presented by them. I also thank co-authors George Demos, Paul Torrance, Norma Jean Groth, Kay Bruch and Charlotte Morrison for the use of material jointly developed.

The following permissions to use copyrighted material are acknowledged with appreciation: *The Journal of Humanistic Psychology*, San Francisco, for permission to use extensive quotes from Dr. Hallman; *The Gifted Child Quarterly*, C. C. Thomas and John Wiley & Sons for permission to use quotations from my writings to which they hold title; the following for shorter quotations from the authors noted: *The Structurist*, Saskatoon (Maslow), Basic Books, N. Y. (Arieti), Coward McCann, N. Y. (Lowen), Farrar, Straus, Giroux, N. Y. (Schneider), Harper & Row, N. Y. (Erikson, Hilgard), Institute of Man, Pittsburgh (Cohn, Sadler, Whalley), International Universities Press, N. Y. (Hitschman), Journal Press, Provincetown (Gutman), Litton Educational Publishing Co., N. Y. (Barron, Flavell), McCall Publishing Co., N. Y. (Spock), John Mann, Livonia, N. Y. (Jourard, Greenwald), W. W. Norton Co., N. Y. (Erikson), *Science & Technology*, Stamford, Conn. (Kubie), University of Kansas Press (Kubie), Van Nostrand Co.,

N. Y. (Barron), and John Wiley & Sons, N. Y. (Getzels, Jackson, Ghiselin, Mogar).

A special acknowledgment is in order to Sybil Richardson, my sometime academic twin, former colleague and constant friend. Her careful editing of the original manuscript exceeded the bounds of mere reading, for many of the less awkward phrasings and more felicitous renderings of half-born ideas are hers. Without her care and attention this book would have been far less lucid, and deep appreciation is extended to her.

Other acknowledgments go to Charles Bish, Carroll Locke, Clifton Winn, Charlotte Malone, and Joyce Sonntag who read the manuscript and made helpful suggestions; to Frances Caldwell who did the figures and diagrams; to Bessie Georgius and Karen Gottfurcht who typed the manuscript and Marilyn Shields who did the indexing; and to my wife Jane who provided the emotional climate which made it possible in the first place.

J. C. G.
Northridge
October, 1971

Development

of the

Creative Individual

1

INTRODUCTION

If man is to become free, he must learn to develop his creativity.

—W. A. Sadler, Jr.

Considering the individual differences among one's fellows with regard to most aspects of physique or personality, one is immediately struck with the fact that (a) the variance is real and (b) its magnitude is ordinarily measured in percentages. Henry may be 20 percent taller than Edward, 30 percent heavier than Jack, and 25 percent brighter than Clyde; but he is unlikely to be twice as tall, as heavy, or as bright as anyone else.

Surprisingly enough this situation does not hold in regard to creativity. On any kind of creative scale used (and creative production of adults is as reliable as any), some individuals are found whose creative production exceeds that of their fellows, not by percentages, or even simple magnitudes; but it is more likely ten, fifty, or a hundred times as great. Obviously these fortunately creative persons are not that much different. Something has happened to turn them on. Creativity is a "threshold" variable. The nature of what that "something" is—the analysis of that threshold—is the task of this book.

Before making this analysis, however, it seems wisest to make a selective search of the literature in regard to development and creativity in order to use

1

some of the ideas and concepts of many others, including major assistance in development from Erikson and Piaget and in creativity from Kubie.

These topics will be taken in order, first proceeding to a search of the literature in regard to development.

THE LITERATURE OF DEVELOPMENT

Development is the noun of the verb "to develop" which among other ways is defined by the *American College Dictionary* as "to bring out the capabilities or possibilities of; to bring to a more advanced or effective state." It is this particular sense that will be pursued here.

In talking about human development, reference may be made to mankind as a species. Development then becomes akin to the forward thrust of evolution which has "developed man from lower form" and (for all we know) may be in the process of developing him into a higher form.

Another sense in which human development is used has to do with the change in the quality of the individual as he progresses through life. This does not mean growth which is change in quantity. A baby is not merely a small adult, and an adult is not usually a large infant. The state and significance of this qualitative change is extremely important.

First consider the literature on each of these species and individual aspects of development in order.

Species Development

It was none other than Condorcet (1795) who said that

> Nature has set no limit to the perfecting of the human faculties; that the perfectability of man is truly indefinite; that the progress of this perfectability, henceforth independent of any power that might wish to arrest it, has no other limit than the duration of the globe on which Nature has placed us.

It is important for scientists to investigate the evolutionary process by which this development occurs. Since this book is not a treatise on biology, a full survey of these facts cannot be undertaken. However, certain aspects of biological theory will be singled out to have a bearing on later discussion.

Among other speculations, one type in particular has stood out as having considerable importance. It is the specifics of development from primate forms into true men.

It was the thesis of the Dutch biologist, Bolk (1926), that man represents the foetalization of the ape. Man does not develop the animal snout, the brow ridges or the heavy jaw. This has been accomplished by a lengthening of the immature period of one species to cover the entire life span of the new species. As a result, there is a great slowing down of various apelike growth processes and a corresponding increase in teachability and trainability of man during this lengthened immaturity and adolescence. This period may cover a third of man's life span, whereas in most animals it is a much smaller period. Even so large a mammal as the whale requires only two years to reach sexual maturity.

To this same point Hardin (1961) states:

> If there is one feature for which man is remarkable among the mammals, it is in his extraordinarily slow maturation. . . . If one compares the face of other mammals, one is struck with the fact that the protruding snout which develops at various degrees of lateness in other animals never develops in man. . . . More important . . . it is the delay in mental maturity in the young, or . . . the prolongation of the teachable period. [p. 257]

Bucke (1929) points out that human beings are just in the process of acquiring some traits or powers. He mentions color and musicality as recently acquired by the race, along with the smell of fragrances, and notes the paucity of descriptions of these in ancient writings. He states (1929)

> Each of our mental faculties has its normal age for appearing in the individual. . . . The longer the race has been in possession of a given faculty the more universal that faculty. . . . The longer the race has been in possession of a given faculty the more firmly is that faculty fixed in each individual who possesses it.
> To sum up: As ontology is nothing but philogeny in petto, the evolution of the individual is the evolution of the race in abridged form. . . . When a new faculty appears in a race it will be found at the very beginning in one individual; later it will be found in a few individuals; after a further time, in a larger percentage. . . . When a new faculty occurs it must appear in members who have reached full maturity. [pp. 45–52]

Individual Development

Consideration will be given much later in this volume to the concept of developmental stages, the central property of which are a series of discrete discontinuities, each having certain characteristics and appearing in a certain order. While this theory has been well enunciated by Erikson (1963) and Piaget (1950), it is important to realize that glimmers of the idea come from other earlier writers.

Emerson (1950) in his essay "The Oversoul" had this to say even a century ago:

> The soul's advances are not made by gradations, such as can be represented by motion in a straight line, but rather by ascension of state, such as can be represented by metamorphosis. . . . The growth of genius is of a certain total character that does not advance the elect individual first over John, then Adam, then Richard . . . but by every throe of growth the man expands there where he works, passing at each pulsation classes, populations of men. [p. 130]

Escalona (1968) states that development reflects increasingly complex adaptation and feels that the alternation between arousal and quiescence stimulates that adaptation. [p. 512] Kubie (1958) came close to the concept of developmental stages in a discussion of the maturation of symbolic processes, for he states that the course of creativity is from chaos to dream to analog to precise concept. [p. 26] This statement is reminiscent of the proverb, "A trace, a path, a lane, a highway."

The difficulty of organizing adult developmental patterns for analytical purposes has been noted by several researchers. Kelly (1955) concluded that, despite the complexities of adult life, there were some valid stability correlations in his longitudinal study and that psychological growth during adulthood is a real possibility. Neugarten (1964), after a careful review of Eriksonian stage theory, did not find evidence of stage shifts by chronological age groups and sought alternative ways of conceptualization. Some, such as Anderson (1956), have embraced choice-point theory; others, such as Charlotte Buhler (1962), have postulated interacting but independent methods of coping which exist simultaneously in the adult, and one of which is dominant. These include (1) active undeveloped mode: need fulfillment; (2) passive undeveloped mode: self-limiting adaptation; (3) active developed mode: creative expansion; and (4) passive developed mode: upholding internal order. Buhler felt that with mental health in adulthood there was a shift toward the third mode, that of creative expansion.

Beggs (1967) has expanded the Buhler concept by adding choice-point theory and postulating that it is at natural choice points (such as a woman whose children are grown taking a new job) that "crossovers" of emphasis or dominance of one system over another changes under the impact of the meeting of the individual's life style and the new environment. Beggs calls this arena of action the "interface," for it is here that one develops different modes of coping. The choice points become the stimuli which escalate individuals into new developmental stages.

Among those who have offered theories of child development, Harry Stack Sullivan (1953) and Robert Sears (1957) should be mentioned prominently. Sullivan's theory, however, is mainly associated with the dynamisms of anxiety since his major preoccupation was with mental disease. Sears, by contrast, considered learning to be the basic force in personality development. A good deal of what Sullivan said is subsumed by Erikson, and what Sears said is subsumed by Piaget. A comparison of the three theories of Erikson, Piaget and Sears is afforded by Maier (1965). In this volume it seemed best to model the analysis on Erikson (1963) and Piaget (1950) as departure points.

It should be noted that Maslow's (1954) hierarchy of basic needs is also a developmental statement. In the original form there were eight stages in the hierarchy: physiological, safety, love, self-esteem, information, understanding, beauty, and self-actualization. These correspond rather well with the Eriksonian eight stages.

The Eriksonian and the Piagetian stages will not be displayed here since much will be made of them in later chapters. It can be pointed out at this time that there is remarkable agreement among the various authorities quoted on personal development. Specifically,

a. Development is different in quality from growth.

b. It consists of stages, in an invariant order.

c. Each stage has characteristic properties different from the rest.

d. The stages are discontinuous.

e. Each stage is in some sense a summation of previous stages.

f. There is an element of escalation or enlargement.

g. There is general agreement as to the approximate age levels.

Sinott, the distinguished biologist, sums up these views on development when he tells us (Anderson, 1959, p. 16):

> Development is not an aimless affair; each stage follows precisely upon its predecessor . . . Continual change is the keynote of this cycle; not unguided change, but change that moves toward a very definite end . . . .

Reich (1970) glimpses the *Zeitgeist* when he remarks: "What Consciousness III represents in the long-range terms of human evolution is the beginning of the development of new capacities in man."

THE LITERATURE OF CREATIVITY

Of all the powers of man, that of creativity seems unique. The generally accepted custom among the ancients was to ascribe divine origin, inspiration or direction to any great creative work so that the poet became the prophet. Even the aspects of initiation and selection, which are universally found in creative function, appear somewhat mysterious, and many of our greater artists and scientists seem to *receive* inspiration rather than to *develop* it.

To create, mind must withdraw upon itself for a time to focus its forces and then project an image of itself onto an external medium. Psychologically this introspection and focusing takes the form of heightened awareness of the peripheral asymmetries of a situation and a subtle settling into consciousness of concepts at the boundaries of rationality or in the preconscious. This is the incubation period in the famous Wallas explication of the four components of creative process: *preparation, incubation, illumination* and *verification*. It is understandable then that the hour of creation is a "tender time" when man wishes to draw apart from his fellows, whether up the mountain, into the desert or away to his closet, but always into a solitary silence. Creative withdrawal and return, as Toynbee has pointed out, is a characteristic of creative acts of groups as well as of individuals.

Because creativity is a word which has recently been taken over by psychology from religion, it is almost impossible to discover it in a dictionary more than a decade old. It is still a new concept, recently attributed to the personality of man, and still to some fraught with mystical connotations. For this reason, care should be taken in defining it and in distinguishing it from other mental functions, as well as to note its possible varieties.[1]

Hallman (1963, pp. 18–19) gave a comprehensive definition:

---

[1] These three paragraphs have been adapted from pp. 66–68 of Gowan, J.C. and Demos, G.D. *The Education and Guidance of the Ablest*, Copyright 1964 by C. C. Thomas Co., Springfield, Ill. Used by permission.

> . . . the creative act can be analyzed into five major components: (1) it is a whole *act*, a unitary instance of behavior; (2) it terminates in the production of *objects* or of forms of living which are distinctive; (3) it evolves out of certain *mental processes*; (4) it co-varies with specific *personality transformations*, and (5) it occurs within a particular kind of *environment*. A demonstration of the necessary features of each of these factors can employ both descriptive and logical procedures; it can refer to the relevance of empirical evidence, and can infer what grounds are logically necessary in order to explain certain facts.[1]

Creativity, like leadership is better defined in terms of interactive process than in terms of trait theory. The creative process in superior adults usually results in creative and useful products. Hence, the creativity of such adults is judged in terms of quantity and quality of patents, theories, books, works of art or music and scientific hypotheses. In children, however, where the product may be original with the child but cannot be original with the culture, assessments of creativity usually depend on nominations of "which child had the most wild or silly ideas" to the more conventional Guilford or Torrance tests of divergent thinking on the child's part. It should be noted here that some researchers have pointed out the fact that there is as yet no proof that this kind of "creativity" on the part of the child will result in the more demonstrable creative production on the part of the adult. In addition, Guilford in particular objects to the term "creativity" as a confusing stereotype of many kinds of ability found in the structure of intellect model and prefers to regard it only as "productive thinking."

Another way of looking at the issues is to analyze the personality correlates or the environmental background which has produced creative adults. This is the method taken by many researchers; notably that of the Institute of Personality Assessment and Research (IPAR) at Berkeley, the biographical of Taylor and the personality psychometrics of Cattell as seen on the *Sixteen Personality Factor Questionnaire*. These methods yield clear results, indicating a particular kind of individual: intelligent, original, independent, open, intuitive, aesthetically sensitive, highly energetic, dominating, possessing a sense of humor and a sense of destiny, and at home with ambiguity and complexity.

Finally, two polar beliefs must be considered. The first is that creative problem solving is a mundane affair, such as knowing how to turn on the lights in a dark room because one knows where the switch is. This, the Osborn-Buffalo view, states that the techniques of creative problem solving can be taught to anyone as a rational and pragmatic affair. The other or psychedelic view holds that creativity is a dawning of the psychedelic powers of man which can transform him from a rational being into a super-rational one through the use of psychedelia, hypnosis, religious or meditational exercises, drugs, mysticism, and what have you. It is as far out as the other is conventional.

In this early analysis of creativity, no clues or theories should be neglected. If creativity were an easy matter, it would have been solved before now. In the

---

[1]This and subsequent quotes from "The Necessary and Sufficient Conditions for Creativity" are reprinted by permission of the author and *The Journal of Humanistic Psychology* 3:1, Spring 1963.

following presentation the available literature is organized into five sections for analysis in terms of a rational-psychedelic continuum.

    a. Cognitive, rational and semantic: problem-solving views of the Buffalo School, the Guilford structure of intellect, and others

    b. Personality and environmental: child-rearing practices, personality correlates, especially originality, energy and high self-concept

    c. Mental health: Rogerian, Maslovian, self-actualization, openness, etc.

    d. Freudian and neo-Freudian: psychoanalytic, oedipal, pleasure, and preconscious

    e. Psychedelic: existential, nonrational, cosmic consciousness, and psychedelic.

Creativity as Cognitive, Rational and Semantic

Attention may now be given to an extremely important group of researchers who have regarded creativity in the main as little else than problem solving. It is a form of rational thought which connects things, which combines parts into new wholes and which (like Sherlock Holmes) performs seeming miracles through observation, insight and meaningful analysis of semantic elements.

Hallman (1963) calls this condition *connectedness* and says that it imposes on man

> . . . the need to create by bringing already existing elements into a distinctive relation to each other. The essence of human creativeness is relational, and an analysis of its nature must refer to the connectedness of whatever elements enter into the creative relationship. The analysis must demonstrate that though man does not create the components, he can nevertheless produce new connections among them. It must prove that these connections are genuinely original and not simply mechanical. Logically, this means that connectedness comprises relationships which are neither symmetrical nor transitive; that is, the newly created connections as wholes are not equivalent to the parts being connected. Neither side of the equation validly implies the other, for the relationship is neither inferential nor causal; rather, it is metaphoric and transformational.

Hallman (1963) calls the roll of some of the writers who have called attention to this aspect of creative performance as follows: Bruner (1962) who states that creativity grows out of combinational activity; Taylor (1964) who points to new organizational patterns; Murray (Anderson, 1959, p. 96 ff.) who finds a compositional process; Ghiselin (1952) who abstracts a new constellation of meanings.

Creativity has also been considered as resulting from particular types of logical thought. This was indeed the view of Osborn (1953) in *Applied Imagination*, and the problem-solving methods he espoused. These go back to Dewey (1910), Rossman (1931) and Wallas (1926) and are found in the practice of the Buffalo Creative Problem-Solving Workshop which Osborn founded and which is carried on by his protege, Parnes (Gowan, Demos and Torrance, 1967, pp. 32–43). Edwards (1968) has supplied us with a survey of creative problem-solving courses.

Hallman (1963) again covers this ground admirably:

> It is generally agreed that creative thought consists of certain integrating synthesizing functions; that it deals with relational forms rather than with individual instances; that it discovers new forms which can accommodate past experiences. It involves a real fusion of forms and not a mere juncturing.

But of all those who have looked at creativity from a rational, problem-solving point of view, certainly the most impressive are the factor analysts. Perhaps it was just the involved statistics that were overpowering; certainly these men, from Spearman through Kelley and Thurstone to Cattell and Guilford, have discussed the subject with an authority and precision scarcely found elsewhere.

It is interesting to note that, whereas now intelligence and creativity are subsumed under wider mental powers called "intellect," the early psychometricians subsumed creativity under intelligence and often tended to depreciate its alleged separate identity. This was true not only of the early unifactorists such as Binet and Terman, but often even of the first multifactorist, Spearman.

Few nowadays would agree with Spearman, who declared in *Abilities of Man* (1931, p. 187), "All creativeness or originality depends solely on eduction of correlates, and is therefore merely a manifestation of general intelligence; no special creative power exists." Although later exponents of such a view have included Thorndike (1966), the general feeling is that creativity and intelligence are different aspects of intellect, or at least are only moderately correlated.

While factor analysts did not discover creativity in the factors of intellect until Guilford's "Structure of Intellect," others were making earlier appraisals of creative process which separated it from intelligence. Some of these efforts tended to equate creativity with problem solving.

Dewey (1910) offered an initial attempt at a problem-solving model for creativity by suggesting the following steps: (1) awareness that a problem exists, (2) analysis of the problem, (3) an understanding of the nature of the problem, (4) suggestions for possible solutions, and (5) testing the alternative solutions and accepting or rejecting them.

Wallas (1926) suggested a somewhat similar model, but with more attempt to account for preconscious aspects: (1) preparation (assembling the information, a long rational process), (2) incubation (temporary relaxation, play or turning the matter over to the preconscious), (3) inspiration (a brief moment of insight), and (4) evaluation (elaboration and testing of the completed process or product).

Rossman (1931) noted that an inventor goes through a similar process and decided on seven steps: (1) observed needs, (2) formulation of problem, (3) available information collected, (4) solution formulated, (5) solutions examined critically, (6) new ideas formulated, and (7) new ideas tested.

Guilford, whose approach has been followed by Gowan and Demos (1967, pp. 193 ff.), asserts that similarities between these models indicate the strong connections between creativity and problem solving. He even regards the mention of incubation in the Wallas model as a "logical error" (1950).

Guilford's positivistic views on creativity (or as he calls it "productive thinking") as simply another cell in the structure of the intellectual model are well explicated in his classic *The Nature of Human Intelligence* (1967) and are too well known to need further explanation here. Despite his other major contributions, Guilford is no developmentalist, and one does not find in his writings an awareness of developmental aspects of the subject, which are so much more prominent in the works of Piaget, Erikson and Rogers, for example.

It was once thought that divergent production carried most of the structure of intellect variance making for creativity, although as early as 1963 (Aschner and Bish, 1965, pp. 5—20), Guilford was arguing for a more expanded view. Recently in a speech at the 1970 Buffalo Creative Problem-Solving Workshop, Guilford indicated that the importance of transformations in creative production has been generally underrated. The five abilities concerned with transformations had the highest average as compared with divergent production in some of his experiments. Even to understand facts, one must be able to transform one's concepts from old to new. Solving problems, therefore, may well depend upon changing one's concept of problems to opportunities—which is a matter of the cognition of semantic transformations. The cognition of semantic implications, or problem sensitivity, as well as the operations of evaluation are other neglected areas feeding into creative production. Transformations, however, are particularly involved when verbal analogies take place, particularly those which involve innovative complexity.

It might be particularly useful to look at the divergent production of semantic transformations (DMT) as being especially loaded with creative content. Appropriately enough, this cell in the structure of intellect is named "originality," namely the production of "effective surprise."

Creativity as Personal and Environmental

The trait and environment theories about creativity have long received considerable attention. There are three main areas of interest:

a. Creativity as a personality correlate, especially of originality, energy, humor and high self-concept

b. Creativity as a result of environment, especially parental rearing practice

c. Creativity as a concomitant of age and stage and other auxiliary variables.

Creativity as a personality correlate has received the main attention. Hallman (1963), in his definitive review, says:

> For example, a large body of evidence has accumulated in connection with the effort to identify the particular *personality traits* which make for creativity. The assumption is that the creative process can be fully accounted for by providing an exhaustive list of such traits. . . . Fromm speaks of four traits: capacity to be puzzled, ability to concentrate, capacity to accept conflict, and willingness to be reborn every day (1959). Rogers has a similar list: openness to experience, internal locus of evaluation, and ability to toy with elements (1959). Maslow has perhaps the most extensive list (1962); the

creative personality, he says, is spontaneous, expressive, effortless, innocent, unfrightened by the unknown or ambiguous, able to accept tentativeness and uncertainty, able to tolerate bipolarity, able to integrate opposites. The creative person is the healthy, self-actualizing person Maslow believes. Others who have identified creative traits are Barron (1963), Meier (1939), Whiting (1958), Angyal (1956), Mooney (1956), Lowenfeld (1958), and Hilgard (1959).

Some typical research results follow. Hilgard says (Anderson, 1959, pp. 175–176):

> I wish to call attention to some immature or childlike qualities manifested among these creative people. Among these qualities I would list are (1) dependency on others, with refusal to accept or carry out the ordinary social responsibilities of adult life, (2) defiance of authority or conventions, (3) a sense of omnipotence, or what Gough has called a sense of destiny, and (4) gullibility, or uncritical acceptance in some intellectual sphere. . . .[1]

Dinkmeyer and Caldwell (1970, p. 89) say, "The child is not only a tension-reducing being but creative as well as reactive. He is motivated by the desire for mastery and self-actualization." Helson (1967) in doctoral research found creative men differed in traits connected with high socioeconomic status, self-awareness, and professional participation. Flescher (Mooney and Razik, 1967) in a creativity-intelligence study with a small number of elementary children found three creativity factors in the ensuing matrix: (1) flexibility fluency, (2) fantasy expression and (3) originality.

Weisberg and Springer (Mooney and Razik, 1967) chose 50 of the most creative and gifted children out of 4000 in the Cincinnati schools and gave them tests and interviews. The five highest judgment categories (all significant at the 5 percent level) following the interview were (1) strength of self-image, (2) ease of early recall, (3) humor, (4) availability of oedipal anxiety and (5) uneven ego development.

Welsh (1967) used an adjective check list on Governor's School students which indicated that high creative adolescents are independent, nonconforming individuals who have change and variety in environment and also have active heterosexual interests.

Whelan (1965) used a theoretical key of seven scales with the following correlations with creativity:

a. energy ($r = .67$): few illnesses, avid reader, early physical development, good grades, active in organizations

b. autonomy ($r = .60$): values privacy, independent, early to leave home

c. confidence ($r = .68$)

d. openness to new experience ($r = .37$)

e. preference for complexity ($r = .13$)

---

[1]From page 175–6, Hilgard, A. in Anderson, H. A. (Ed.) *Creativity and Its Cultivation,* Copyright 1959, Harper & Row Publishers. Used by permission.

f. lack of close emotional ties (r = .30)

g. permissive value structure (r = .67).

Hallman (1963, pp. 20–21) states:

> Descriptively, the second criterion can be called the condition of origi-
> nality ... This category specifies four qualities which any item must have if it
> is to exist as an ideographic, non-classifiable object, that is if it is to be genu-
> inely original. These are novelty, unpredictability, uniqueness, and surprise ...
> First then, novelty means newness, freshness, inventiveness; it is universally
> recognized by writers in the field as an indispensable quality of originality.

Dellas and Gaier (1970) reviewed creativity research on five variables: (1) intellectual factors, (2) intelligence, (3) personality, (4) potential creativity and (5) motivational characteristics. Creative persons appear more distinguished by interests, attitudes and drives rather than high intelligence. Creativity seems to be a synergic effect involving cognitive style, openness and other personality variables.

Neither permissiveness, overindulgence, nor a great deal of love in the home appears to stimulate creative performance as had, in some quarters, been alleged; but a good deal of parental interaction with children, plus authoritative (not authoritarian) behavior on the part of the parents, appears helpful. The mixed results make it appear that parental rearing practices and other environmental influences are not central in producing creative persons, at least not so much so as individual personality dynamics. Some research results follow.

Hitschman (1956, p. 19), in a study of "great men," noted that

> Several subjects show a traumatic experience in early childhood as a pos-
> sible source of their creativity. All were excessively day-dreamers. Many showed
> a certain bisexuality or femininity or at least some conflict in masculine-
> feminine identification. Their productivity can be compared to an act of
> childbirth.[1]

There have been a number of doctoral dissertations focusing on relationships between home environment and personality factors on the one hand and creativity on the other. Abdel-Salan (1963) found the male adolescent creative, self-sufficient, alternately lax and exacting and a trusting, adaptable, surgent, easy-going cyclotheme. Ellinger (1964) obtained a correlation of .6 between creativity and home environment for 450 fourth graders. Parents of creative children were more involved in activities, read more to children, went more often out to the library and used less physical punishment. Orinstein (1961), using the PARI, found maternal restrictiveness correlated .4 with low vocabulary, but neither permissiveness nor loving attitude correlated with creativity. Pankove (1966) found a positive relationship between creativity and risk-taking boys.

---

[1]From page 19, Hitschman, E. *Great Men*, Copyright 1956, International Universities Press, New York. Used by permission.

Arasteh (1968) concluded, after a careful survey of creativity in young children, that a loving, authoritative but somewhat permissive family structure was more productive of creative children than an autocratic or inflexible one.

Torrance (1969), in reporting intercultural research in which the author also participated (Gowan and Torrance, 1963), found strong relationships between cultural environment and creative index.

Research in which the author participated (Gowan and Torrance, 1965; Torrance, Gowan, Wu and Aliotti, 1970) indicates that in cross cultural studies of creative performance in children, strain is put upon the child with resultant reduction in creativity by bilingualism at home or school.

Coone (1968), in doctoral research under Torrance using a cross-cultural study, found the fourth grade drop in creativity confined to American culture.

Datta and Parloff (1967) attempted to determine the kind of family in which the creative individual is likely to develop. Previous studies indicated that the relevant dimension is autonomy control. Both creative scientists and their less creative controls described parents as moderately affectionate, nonrejecting and encouraging. The creatives were more likely to perceive parents as providing a "no rules" situation in which their integrity, autonomy and responsibility were taken for granted.

A third area, that of age and stage aspects of creativity, was also researched. The effects of age on creativity have been studied in superior adults by Botwinick (1967) and by Lehman (Botwinick, 1967; Lehman, 1953, 1960). Their findings generally agree that creativity is more often found in younger individuals, and that young men in their twenties are especially apt to be highly innovative in science. A somewhat later apex is found for the behavioral sciences, but the peak of creative performance seems passed by the age of forty. Similar results had been reported earlier by Bjorkstein (1946).

Hallman (1963) in his definitive review says:

> Another body of data has been collected to prove that creativity can be fully explained as a series of chronological stages, each stage of which makes its unique contribution to the total process. Wallas (1926) provides the classical statement of this position, and he has been followed by Patrick (1937) and Spender (1946) in connections with creativeness in poetry; Hadamard (1954) and Poincare (1913) in mathematics; Arnold (1959), Patrick and Montmasson (1931) in science. Others who define creativity in terms of serial stages are Ghiselin (1952), Vinacke (1952) and Hutchinson (1949).

Solomon (1968), in doctoral research, found some rather complex relationships between creativity as measured by the Torrance tests and SES, but none between creativity and intelligence.

Among others who found high SES a factor in children's creativity was Saveca (1965) in a cross cultural study, and Feld (1968), who concluded after doctoral research that intelligence and age accounted for 30 percent of the variance in creativity scores, and personality factors for another 30 percent. Tibbets (1968) concluded—after doctoral research that, of socioeconomic status, race, sex, intelligence, age and grade point average in a heterogeneous group of adolescents, intelligence and race were the best predictors of creativity.

Creativity as Mental Health and Openness

A large and prestigious group of researchers, including Jung (Arieti, 1967), Maslow (1954) and Rogers (1959) to name only three, associate creative functioning with a high degree of mental health, openness to experience, and antiauthoritarian influences and tendencies in the individual style of living. Maslow's classic chapter, "Self-Actualizing People: A Study of Psychological Health" (1954), contains in its title a strong affirmation of relationship; moreover the common qualities he finds in his survey include spontaneity, autonomy, democratic (antiauthoritarian) character structure, and of course, creativity. Rogers (1959), who equates the goals of psychotherapy with "openness to experience," "an internal locus of evaluation," and "ability to toy with concepts," believes these are the same conditions most associated with creativity within the individual. Schachtel (1959) speaks of the quality of the encounter which develops into creative performance as primarily one of openness.

Hallman (1963), in his thorough review, also names openness and says:

> It designates those characteristics of the environment, both the inner and the outer, the personal and the social, which facilitates the creative person's moving from the actual state of affairs which he is in at a given time toward solutions which are only possible and as yet undetermined. These conditions, or traits, include sensitivity, tolerance of ambiguity, self-acceptance, and spontaneity. Since these are passively rather than actively engaged in the creative process, this criterion may be explained logically within the category of *possibility*. But again, the psychological meaning of this category may best be expressed under the concept of deferment, as distinguished, for example, from closure; of postponement as distinguished from predetermined solutions.

Schulman (1966) found openness of perception necessary for creative functioning.

Openness can be described in twelve aspects, all mentioned by Maslow (1954) as characteristic of his group of self-actualized people. The first four aspects are also noted by Hallman.

(1) *Problem sensitivity* refers to the ability to sense things as they might be reassembled, to a discrepancy, an aperture or a hiatus. It involves a particular kind of openness which divines that things are not quite what they seem. Hallman cites Angyal (1956), Fromm (1959), Guilford (1967), Greenacre (1957), Hilgard (1959), Lowenfeld (1958), Mooney (1956) and Stein (1953) as witnesses for the importance of problem sensitivity in creative performance.

(2) *Ability to tolerate ambiguity* is another aspect widely noted. Hallman (1963) characterizes it as "the ability to accept conflict and tension resulting from polarity (Fromm, 1959), to tolerate inconsistencies and contradictions (Maslow, 1963), to accept the unknown, and be comfortable with the ambiguous, approximate, and uncertain." He names Hart (1950), Wilson (1954) and Zilboorg (1959) as holding similar views. The ability to tolerate ambiguity appears also related with two other aspects. One is the ability to toy with ideas, rather playfully rearranging them into different forms. The other is preference for complexity, found by Barron (1963) in his study of artists.

(3) *Internalized locus of evaluation* is a Rogerian phrase for what Hallman calls a sense of destiny and personal worth which internalizes the value system so that it is not dependent upon cultural mores. This personal autonomy, also named by Maslow (1954) as characteristic of self-actualized people is really the opposite of authoritarian tendencies. The development of autonomy in young adults has been found to be negatively correlated with authoritarianism. Benton (1967), in a doctoral thesis, found openness (opposite of authoritarianism) to be predictive of creativity among students. An interesting sidelight of this aspect is the resultant philosophical, unhostile sense of humor, so characteristic of creative people, and found by Maslow as one of the qualities of his self-actualized group.

(4) *Spontaneity* is a quality used by both Hallman and Maslow to describe openness and creativity. It involves more isomorphic and comfortable relations with reality, so that one experiences life directly and "openly," not as if through a darkened glass. There is an appreciation and wonderment toward life, a childlike awe and admiration of that which is mysterious about the universe, blending into a mystic or oceanic feeling. All of these are qualities named by Maslow about his self-actualized people. "Scientific genius," said Poincare, "is the capacity to be surprised."

Finally, while still on the mental health aspect of creativity, the considerable testimony should be noted for creativity as at least a two-stage process as one ascends the mental health scale. Arieti (1967, p. 335) describes Jung's views as follows:

> Jung believes that the creative process occurs in two modes: the psychological and the visionary; the first mode nowhere transcends the bounds of psychological intelligibility. In the visionary mode, which concerns Jung more deeply, the content emerges from the collective unconscious . . . The creative process then consists of an unconscious animation of the archetype, and hence the great works of art transcend life experience of the period in which its producer lives, and is conferred with universal significance.[1]

Hallman (1963), in his definitive review, has this to say:

> A third cluster of evidence surrounds the definition that creative activity involves an interchange of energy among *vertical layers* of psychological systems. Creativeness consists in a shift of psychic levels. Most writers identify two psychological levels and refer to them variously as the primary-secondary processes, the autistic and reality adjusted, unconscious mechanisms and conscious deliberation, free and bound energies, gestalt-free and articulating tendencies. These writers include Freud, Ehrenzweig (1953), and Schneider (1950). Maslow (1959) adds to these two levels a third one called integration.

Another who believes in two levels of creativity is Taft (1970), who states:

> There are two styles of creativity; one a measured, problem-solving approach, and the other an emotion and comparatively uncontrolled free expression.

---

[1]From page 335, Arieti, S. *The Intrapsychic Self*, Copyright 1967, Basic Books, New York. Used by permission.

Taft believes that this dichotomy stems from the distinction made between primary and secondary processes by Freud. The primary process creativity (or "hot" creativity) occurs in the preconscious, and the secondary process (or "cold" creativity) requires more controls and less fantasy expression, such as scientific investigation, for example.

And Ghiselin (Taylor and Barron, 1963, p. 42) tells us that

> It is reasonable to say that there are two levels of creaitity, one higher and one lower, one primary and one secondary, one major and one minor. Creative action of the lower, secondary sort gives further development to an established body of meaning through initiating some advance in its use . . . . Creative action of the higher, primary sort alters the universe of meaning itself, by introducing into it some new element of meaning or some new order of significance, or, more commonly, both.[1]

Damm (1970) after analyzing studies of Arnold (1962), Blatt (1964), MacKinnon (1964), Barron (1963), Roe (1963) and Gerber (1965) on the relationship between creativity and mental health in adults concludes that a strong relationship exists. Damm (1970) found students high in intelligence and creativity are more self-actualized as measured by Shostrom's (1966) *Personal Orientation Inventory* than students who are high in intelligence only. He concluded that students who obtained high scores on both areas were superior in self-actualization and recommended that the development of both intelligence and creative abilities should be a prime educational goal.

Hallman (1963), speaking about self-actualization, says

> Empirically, this criterion is supported by the great wealth of data which has been reported. Maslow (1956) has spoken most forcefully on this theme. He equates creativity with the state of psychological health, and this with the self-actualization process. There is no exception to this rule, he says. "Creativity is an universal characteristic of self-actualizing people." This form of creativeness reaches beyond special-talent creativeness; it is a fundamental characteristic of human nature. It touches whatever activity the healthy person is engaged in.

Craig (1966) reviewed trait theories of creativity and listed four personality correlates which were congruent with Maslow's holistic scheme of self-actualization and character integration. Newton (1968) in doctoral research found high correlation between progress toward self-actualization and intelligence.

Moustakas (1967) attempted to conceptualize creativity in terms of self-growth and self-renewal by stressing the uniqueness of the individual and his potentialities for mental health.

Creativity as Freudian and Neo-Freudian

The Freudian school. While Freud said comparatively little about creativity as such, psychoanalytic literature has been especially fertile in developing models to account for it. These theories, as pointed out by Hallman (Gowan and Demos,

[1]From pages 42–3, Ghiselin in Taylor, C. W. and Barron, F. (Eds.) *Scientific Creativity: Its Recognition and Development*, Copyright 1963, John Wiley & Sons. Used by permission.

1967) center around several related viewpoints. They start with a number of rather strict followers of the Freudian school including Brill (1931), Deri (1939), Engleman (1952), Erikson (1963), McAlpine and Hunter (1952), Schachtel (1959), Sterba, P. and E. (1952), Van Der Sterren (1952), and Weiss (1953). Freud claimed (1938) that the sublimation of the sexual urge "forms one of the sources of artistic activity," and is the main source of cultural energy, and hence it is not surprising that there is a rather large literature by neo-Freudians linking psychoanalytic theory with artistic enterprise.

For example, Schneider (1950, p. 93) points out that creativity's thrust from the unconscious and creative mastery by the conscious must be joined in the artist, and additionally states:

> The true creative man, to use Freud's phrase, has more at his disposal, special gifts, which enable him to adventure beyond the borders of the corridor of transformation—into the mysteries and mechanics of the process which impinges upon him from the inner time-space world of reality. He lives nearer to his dreams and at the same time he encompasses routine and penetrates beyond routine into the practical magic of ever-changing, ever-subtle reality.[1]

Rank's views. Secondly, come Freud's three great disciples, each of whom rejected some aspect of Freud's sexual explanation of energy transformation in favor of something more positive and grandiose, such as "life-force," compensation, collective unconscious, etc. (Adler, 1952; Jung, 1916; and Rank, 1932).

Otto Rank was one of the first to extend psychoanalytic theory to cover creative production. Defining will as the integration of self-concept, he made it a central issue in the ego-psychology which he developed. Rank saw man as moving through existence from the trauma of the womb to the trauma of the tomb, beset with two fundamental fears—fear of life, and fear of death. Fear of life is fear of differentiation, of separation, of being oneself. Since it is the fear of independence, it causes regression to symbolic union with the mother figure. Fear of death is fear of integration, of joining with others, of having one's personality lost. Fear of life drives man to union with others; fear of death drives one to an assertion of oneself. Rank saw the measurement of development in an individual as the degree to which he achieves a constructive integration of these two polar opposites in his nature.

Specifically, will is first experienced as a negative counter to parental demands during the autonomy period, and it causes guilt and immobilization during the initiative period. Some children give up the fight right here; they decide never to oppose parental will, and by extension adapt wholeheartedly to the laws of school and society. These become the *adapted* type—bland, placid, conforming, and sterile. It is the easiest solution to the problem, but at the price of lost creativeness. Then there are those who wage uncertain warfare in this area. They are more or less bound by parental and societal demands, yet they have not given up completely, and while suffering pangs of conscience, are not completely guilt immobilized. The price they pay for this ambivalence and lack of resolution is neuroticism.

---

[1]From page 93, Daniel E. Schneider, *The Psychoanalyst and the Artist*, Copyright 1950, Farrar, Straus & Giroux, Inc., New York. Used by permission.

This is the condition of "civilized" man, at war with himself, as he is with social forces around him. This type, according to Rank, has at least progressed from the adapted type, so that he may be said to be "on the way," but until the neurotic problem has been allayed, his creative gifts are generally denied and remain latent. The third type, more progressed than the other two, is, in Rank's view, the true creative artist, a man of "will and deed." He is imaginative and has the energy and thrust to get his ideas accomplished.[1]

The neo-Freudians. Third come a group of writers who adopt the neo-Freudian view that the oedipal crisis during the narcissistic period is the genesis of creative function. These include Besdine (1968, 1970), Gowan (1965), Kubie (1958), Ruitenbeek (1965), and Winnicott (1965). Besdine (1970), for example, finds a particular style of mothering contributes to the development of creativity in the child. The intelligent mother's need for emotional intimacy and intellectual contact with an only child or oldest son results in an intense mother-child attachment. This feminizes the son, but opens up for him more idea striving, more imagination, and more interest in literature and art.

Gowan (1965, pp. 3–6) described the child's oedipal response to the affectional approach of the opposite-sexed parent as an original theory according to which

> . . . boys who were close to their mothers and girls close to their fathers during the period between four and seven will become more creative than others. Such a theory, of course, would explain why there appear to be more creative men than women in the world. The child, at this time, enchanted by the warm effect of the opposite-sexed parent, responds to this in the only way he can—by the creative manipulation of his immediate environment, and by the enlargement of the bridge between his fantasy life and his real world.[2]

Attempting to verify this theory by means of questionnaires to parents of creative and noncreative, gifted children, Gowan (1969) found that "the opposite-sexed parent had devoted more time to this child than the same sexed parent" favored high creatives over low creatives by a score of 11 to 5, and the child was declared very close to the opposite-sexed parent by a score of 20 to 11.

Another research finding indicating that warmth in the opposite-sexed parent promotes creativity in the young child was that of Pauline Sears (1968), who, in a carefully delineated study, found definite indications of the influence of this affective warmth on creative development.

Singer (1961) found her high fantasy children showed significantly greater oedipal involvement as opposed to preoedipal conflict in the low fantasy group. Weisberg and Springer (1961) report creative children reveal their oedipal anxieties more easily than noncreative. Greenacre (1957) found that gifted children resolved their oedipal problems less decisively. Helson (1967), who investigated some especially creative college women, reported there was some tendency for

---

[1]Rank's views on creativity were included in the remarks by Dr. Donald MacKinnon at the Buffalo Creative Problem-Solving Workshop in June 1970.

[2]From Gowan, J. C. "What Makes a Gifted Child Creative: Four Theories" *Gifted Child Quarterly*, 9:3–6, 1965. Used by permission.

them as daughters to model themselves on their fathers to a greater extent than among the less creative group. Schaefer (1970), in another study on especially creative adolescent girls, suggests that his creative subjects have identified more with the father than the mother and notes several results of his analysis which support this conclusion.

Oedipal theories. A variation of this oedipal theme is that creative accomplishments are sublimations of aggressive, phallic or incestuous desires and hence refinements of basic drives and primary process. Among those holding such views are numbered Fairburn (1938), Grotjohan (1957), Levey (1940), Schneider (1950), Segal (1952), Simon and Gagnon (1969), Sharp (1930) and Spock (1970). Schneider sees creativity as the outcome of phallic thrust and mastery stemming from the Freudian narcissistic period, while Simon and Gagnon (1969) wonder if the erotic fantasies accompanying masturbation do not help boys catch up with girls in measures of achievement and creativity. A view more in line with Puritan ethos values is taken by famed pediatrician Benjamin Spock who says:

> Though the pressure of the physical aspect of sexuality is intense in adolescence, part of it is still held in check and transformed into idealistic channels, to the degree that the family has aspirations. In such families, the little boy's romantic adoration of his mother, suppressed for years, veiled, disembodied, now lends depth, mystery, and spirituality to his awakening love for a girl. . . . This idealization of women is a source of further inspiration to men. It combines with their drive to create, and these two forces are the principal sources of men's poetry, novels, plays, music, painting, sculpture, much of which has women as its subject. . . . The biographies of a number of remarkably creative men show that as boys they were inspired to an unusual degree by the characters of their mothers, and by the fantasies, ambitions and ideals their mothers kindled in them.[1]

The preconscious. Finally, there are those who regard the preconscious as the sources of man's creativity and its development as central. These include principally Kubie (1958) in his masterly treatise, "The Neurotic Distortion of the Creative Process," but also Happich (1932), Kris (1952) and Getzels and Jackson (1962) and the present writer.

Getzels and Jackson (1962) attempt to explain this effect in terms of the theory of Kubie (1958), "pointing to the greater flux or movement of preconscious material into the conscious expression of the creative person." They note more impulsive, unusual responses concerning vocational choices and other interests, which diverge from stereotyped meanings in the creative as contrasted with the noncreative. They quote Schachtel (1959, p. 243) as stating that creative behavior is the "product of repressed libidinal or aggressive impulse and of a regression to infantile modes of thought or experience, to the primary process, albeit in the service of the ego." They quote Freud's initial hypothesis that "creative behavior is a continuation of a substitution for the play of childhood." Kubie speaks of toying with preconscious material, and Bruner (1966) describes

---

[1]From page 34–5, Spock, B. *Decent & Indecent*, Copyright 1970, McCall Publishing Co., New York. Used by permission.

the importance of play first as "an attitude in which the child learns that the outcomes of various activities are not so extreme as he had either hoped or feared." Noting that he has been struck by differences in the encouragement of play in their children by parents, he concludes by arguing that "play makes it possible for intrinsic learning to begin."

Happich (1932) took the level of consciousness he called "symbolic consciousness," which seemed to lie between consciousness and unconsciousness, as the point of departure for all creative production, and therefore also for the healing process. On this level the collective unconscious can express itself through symbolism.

Thus Gutman (Mooney and Razik, 1967, p. 24) states,

> A spontaneous, involuntary, automatic quality of creative thinking processes has been reported by Hadamard (1949). According to Ghiselin (1952), this quality has been experienced by Spencer, Nietzsche, Gauss, Poincare, Henry James, and others. In some, this feeling of automatism has been so strong that it was accompanied by an impression that some outside agent had whispered to them the productive ideas which suddenly came to them. Socrates' "demon" is a famous example.
>
> That creative thinking involves subconscious or nonverbal activity is reported almost universally. Rossman (1931, p. 86), who has made an extensive survey of the traits and working methods of inventors, reports that "many inventors attribute the formation of the mental patterns to the subconscious mind." Hadamard (1954), who has studied the psychology of invention in great mathematicians, quotes Poincare and Einstein in support of the claim that creative thinking involves subconscious or nonverbal mental activity. Evidence for this claim is also given by Maier (1931) in his studies on problem-solving. Ghiselin (1952) comes to the conclusion that "the first impulse toward new order in the psychic life . . . is an impulse away from the conscious activity . . . an impulse toward unconsciousness."

Schneider (1950) points out this barrage of the preconscious by external forces serves to bring down creative performance in the following passage:

> The external world helps the internal inhibition to cut down the preconscious instrument of transformation until it is either stereotyped and rigid, or inert and blocked, instead of having that practiced sensitivity and that elasticity which is of the essence in creative life.[1]

Sadler (1969) equates play and creative perception. He notes that Piaget sees play primarily as the function of assimilation, but it cannot be subsumed entirely under that function. "The underlying structure of play is constituted by a certain reorientation of the ego to reality."

Weissman (1967) reviewed the literature on the Kris idea of creativity as regression in the service of the ego and found it wanting as a valid concept.

Ruth Cohn (Otto and Mann, 1969, p. 177) puts the relationship thus:

---

[1]From page 131, Schneider, S. E. *The Psychoanalyst and the Artist*, Copyright 1950, by Farrar, Straus & Giroux, Inc., New York. Used by permission.

[2]From page 24, Mooney, R. L. and Razik, T. A. *Explorations in Creativity*, Copyright, 1967 by Harper & Row, New York. Used by permission.

Valid intuition uses preconscious roads and sensory, logical and emotional vehicles to connect conscious and unconscious psychological data and organize them.[1]

Kubie (Mooney and Razik, 1967, pp. 33–43) says,

At the core of this process is a continuous stream of subliminal, i.e., "preconscious," activity which goes on both during sleep and when we are awake and is carried on without conscious symbolic imagery. Analogous to a computer it processes "bits" of information by scanning, ordering, selecting and rejecting, arranging in sequence by juxtaposition and separation on the basis of chronology, by condensations on the basis of similarity, dissimilarity by contrasts, proximity and distance and finally summating and coding.

The problem of how to protect the freedom of the preconscious processing in learning in education in general and in creativity.

Again Kubie (Mooney and Razik, 1967, p. 38), having described the demands of the conscious mind and drives of the unconscious, says

How then do creative processes operate between these two rigid systems? This depends upon the freedom of preconscious functions. This is the implement of all thinking, particularly of creative thought. Preconsciously, we process many things at a time. By processes of free associations, we take ideas and approximate realities apart and make swift condensations of their multiple allegorical and emotional import. Preconscious processes make free use of analogy and allegory, superimposing dissimilar ingredients into new perceptual and conceptual patterns, thus reshuffling experience to achieve that extraordinary degree of condensation without which creativity in any field would be impossible.[2]

Gowan (1969) summed up this stance as follows:

We agree with Kubie (1958, p. 50) that creative performance involves "cogitation and intelligence," cogitation, to shake ideas together and intelligence, to select from among ideas. The necessary condition is intelligence which provides the vocabulary to be sorted and the means of selection. We guess, for example, that one reason why children of lower intelligence rarely become creative is that they do not reach Bruner's level of symbolic representation (when ideas become intellectually negotiable because one can recount experience) until nearly the end of the initiative period. In contrast the bright child reaches this stage about the middle of this period when the creative motivations we have discussed can cogitate or "shake together" the symbolic representations of experience. We feel that the Freudian-Eriksonian views heretofore expressed, while sufficient to explain the motivations which produce the cogitation, require amplification of cognitive structure theory to ensure that the shaking up produces something cognitively creative instead of triviality. (The preconsciousness of musical and mathematical genius shows that it is easier for the child to accomplish this in nonverbal than in verbal areas.) We attach importance to the fact that in the Piagetian cognitive stages, the same

---

[1]From page 177, Ruth Cohn in Otto, H. and Mann, J. *Ways of Growth*, Copyright 1968, by Otto & Mann. Used by permission.

[2]From Kubie, L. S. "Blocks to Creativity," Copyright June 1965, *International Science & Technology*. Used by permission (as quoted by Mooney, R. and Razik, T. (Editors) *Explorations in Creativity*. New York: Harper & Row, 1967, pp. 33–43).

age period is named the "intuitive stage." It is quite possible that further developmental discoveries await us in this area.[1]

Another Freudian view sees creativity as an outgrowth of libido pleasure. Lowen (1970) states, "If the bodily pleasure of an individual is destroyed, he becomes an angry, frustrated and hateful person. His thinking becomes distorted, and his creative potential is lost. He develops self-destructive tendencies."[2] Lowen sees pleasure as the source of creativity.

Margolies and Litt (1966), in a study of creativity in art, attempted to explain creativity on theorgonomy theories of William Reich. Hallman (1966), in an evaluation of the aesthetic pleasingness of the creative process, listed four modes of pleasure: suspense, release, elation and delight.

Creativity as Psychedelic

Finally there are those who regard creativity as a psychedelic manifestation, part of the existential "Eigenwelt," or in other paranormal terms. Merely because this stance is less "scientific" than others is no reason to reject it out of hand. The connection of creativity with hypnotism, ESP, and other paranormal aspects by Krippner and others deserves the most careful scrutiny. Among the best sources of this psychedelic aspect are the new books by Tart (1969) and by Masters and Houston (1966), both of which incline to this view.

Psychologists and Freudians tend to place this focus within the human mind, particularly in the preconscious and unconscious aspects; mystics and others are inclined to place it outside, or at least to ascribe outside connections to, or influences on, the preconscious. Since we know so little about the preconscious, both sides deserve a hearing.

Myers (1903), following Janet and Freud, developed a theory of the "subliminal self." He regarded the conscious self as but "a limited and specialized phase of the total self" (Tyrell, 1947, p. 26). It was as Myers (1903, p. 25) put it, "a gold mine as well as a rubbish heap . . . full of upheavals and alternations . . . of many kinds, so that what was once below the surface may for a time . . . rise above it."

It was Tyrell who reminds us that those products of the human mind at once most original and eminent have not come from the realm of consciousness. Rather they have seeped, flowed, or burst into it from beyond (in the preconscious). He then quotes Harding (1942, pp. 68 ff.) on some testimony from famous sources. Socrates is quoted as saying "It is not by wisdom that poets create . . . but by inspiration, like prophets. . . ."

"Poetry is not like reasoning," declared Shelley, "a power to be exerted according to the determination of the will. A man cannot say, 'I will write poetry.' The greatest poet even cannot say it." Blake said of his poem *Milton*, "I have

---

[1]From Gowan, J. C. "Why Some Gifted Children are Creative," *Gifted Child Quarterly,* 15:13–19, Spring 1971. Used by permission.

[2]From Lowen, Alex. *Pleasure,* Copyright 1970, Coward-McCann. Used by permission.

written this poem from immediate dictation . . . without premeditation, and even against my will." Keats remarked that his poetry often came to him "by chance or magic, to be, as it were, something given to him"; and George Eliot confided that in her best writing there was a "not herself." George Sand wrote that "It is *the other* who sings as he likes." Goethe said, "The songs made me, not I them." What is true of poets and writers is also true of scientists and composers—all tell of venturing into an enlarged realm of consciousness as if the Sullivanian "not me" had opened up to them and disgorged a creative fantasy instead of its usual magic nightmare. Psychologically this uncanny "not me" area can be identified as part of the preconscious, containing like the cave of Aladdin marvelous treasure as well as frightening genies. The conscious mind exploring this cavern finds itself overwhelmed by becoming cognizant of an enlarged domain.

Hallman (1963) says of this aspect,

> The incubation stage, for example, consists of spontaneous, uncontrollable events which cluster themselves seemingly in accordance with their own autonomous laws. It involves the relaxation of conscious thinking operations and the inhibitions of logical control. Maslow refers to this process as voluntary regression (1958), Ehrenzweig as surrender of the ego (1953), and Rogers as openness to experience (1959). The stage of illumination remains even more of a mystery. Being singular, unpredictable, idiosyncratic, it resists formal description. Writers from Plato to Lu Chi, in ancient China, to Nietzsche have remarked about the unexplainable nature of inspiration. Patrick has been most diligent in trying to prove the theory of four stages (1937). Poincare and Hadamard (1940) agree that the four stages adequately account for mathematics creations. Arnold (1959), Patrick and Montmasson (1931) discover the same four stages in connection with scientific inventions. Patrick (1937) and Spender (1946) believe that poetic creativeness occurs in sequential stages. Other writers who explain the creative process in this fashion were mentioned above (Vinacke, 1952).

Kierkegaard's name for self-conscious decision making was *Existenz*. It is the self-attitude of the individual called forth by necessity of choice making and, therefore, an inner and self-conscious process of becoming. Or in Sechi's words (1969), "It is a process of creative striving to reaffirm one's commitment to objective possibilities; it is a projection of oneself toward the future. Man's *Existenz* separates thought and being, necessity and freedom, time and eternity, holding them apart from the other in succession."

May pointed out (Anderson, 1959, p. 56) that most psychoanalytic theories about creativity are "reductive," i.e., creativity is reduced to some other process (such as Adler's theory that creativity is seen as an expression of some neurotic pattern; "Regression in service of the ego" is Kris' famous phrase). May goes on to point out that Webster defines creativity as the "process of making or bringing into being" and this aspect of becoming leads May to label creativity as central in existential theory. Creativity, he summarizes, is the encounter of the intensely conscious human being with his world.

Helder, in doctoral research (1968), contrasted mystical and peak experiences found in the more open creative stance with traditional perceptual-cognitive consciousness. Moriarty and Murphy (1967) in research connecting creativity with paranormal experience described five personality variables favorable to both effects. Horonton (1967) in another study of precognition and creativity found that high creatives were much more precognitive than low creatives. Pang and Fort (1967) also investigated the positive correlation between creativity and ESP.

In the opening words of his treatise on "The Creativeness of Life," Edmund Sinott, distinguished biologist, put the matter very succinctly:

> Alfred North Whitehead once remarked that the psychical is the creative advance into novelty. Ralph Lillie (1945) still went further. "Inertia," said he, "is primarily a physical property, a correlate of the conservation which is a recognized character of the physical as physical. In contrast, the psychical, being a factor of novelty, is the *anticonservative* property in nature." In other words, mind is the source of creativity.

SUMMARY

In this introductory chapter an attempt has been made to develop a selective search of the literature in regard to the two major aspects of the title of this volume: development and creativity.

Development has been analyzed as both species improvement and change through evolution, and of personal growth and change to become more effective as an adult. In particular the stage aspects of development have been emphasized, and its qualitative difference from growth noted.

With regard to creativity, where the recent literature has been most prolific, five subdivisions have been recognized on a parameter which goes along a continuum from rational problem solving to irrational psychedelia. These have been categorized as:

a. Cognitive, rational and problem-solving aspects

b. Personality traits, family and environmental origins

c. Mental health, psychological openness and self-actualization

d. Freudian, oedipal and preconscious views

e. Existential, psychedelic and irrational aspects.

2

DEVELOPMENTAL STAGES

All the world's a stage,
And all the men and women merely players . . . .
At first the infant. . . .
Then the whining schoolboy. . . .
And then the lover,
Sighing like a furnace, with a woeful ballad
Made to his mistress' eyebrows. Then a soldier,
Full of strange oaths and bearded like the pard,
Jealous in honor, sudden and quick in quarrel,
Seeking the bubble Reputation
E'en in the cannon's mouth. And then the justice,
In fair round belly with good capon lin'd,
With eyes, severe and beard of formal cut,
Full of wise saws and modern instances;
And so he plays his part. The sixth age shifts
Into the lean and slipper'd pantaloon,
With spectacles on nose and pouch on side;
His youthful hose well sav'd, a world too wide
For his shrunk shank, and his big manly voice,
Turning again toward childish treble, pipes
And whistles in his sound. Last scene of all,
That ends this strange eventful history,
Is second childishness and mere oblivion—
Sans teeth, sans eyes, sans taste, sans everything.

—Shakespeare, *As You Like It,* Act II

The ideas that poets glimpse and geniuses utter require a long time for the world to comprehend and use. Almost 400 years ago, Shakespeare spoke of the seven ages of man, and nearly a century ago, Freud pointed out five developmental periods of sexual libido. Despite the added insights of Erikson and Piaget, educators have been slow to realize that the theory of developmental stages provides the organizing focus for the field of educational psychology. Blocher in writing *Developmental Guidance* (1966) was one of the first to realize and apply this insight to the problems of counseling. It is the thesis of this chapter that the theory of developmental stages, when fully understood and accepted, will synthesize many now disparate aspects of the discipline, and will help to identify the growing stage of educational psychology with more clarity and resolution.

DEVELOPMENT AS A PARAMETER WITH DISCRETE LEVELS

We have been accustomed to thinking of development as if it behaved like growth—a smooth progression on an old-fashioned S-curve. But newer research suggests that this is not so; that instead, development is like a Fourier series, or a flight of locks, namely a staircase-like parameter of hierarchial nature with discrete levels. Now a parameter is a variable which takes on only a relatively small number of values, roughly spaced equally apart. Let us see how this model fits developmental process.

Stated in other words, our task is to determine the nature and direction of developmental change. But this change involves more than mere growth, for development is to growth as quality is to quantity. The apple enlarges, but it also ripens. We see this transformation clearly in the changes wrought by sexual maturation, but there are several other examples of developmental change, each important in forming the adult individual.

Lewin left our discipline a valuable tradition in borrowing so freely from the models of physical science. In understanding the principles of energy transformations, it may be useful to follow his lead and to consider an analogous situation from physics involving latent heat. Assume that we have one gram of water at -100° C. We add 100 calories and heat it to 0° C, but it does not unfreeze from its icy form. To change to water will take 80 more calories, which is known as the latent heat of fusion. The 80 calories are applied and we now have water at 0° C. One hundred more calories are applied, and the water now heats to 100° C, but it does not become steam. To effect that, 540 more calories must be applied to change water from the liquid to the gaseous state. We apply 540 more calories and our water now vaporizes. In raising the ice from -100° C to steam at 100° C, we have applied 200 calories to change temperature and 620 calories to change the state or form of the material, an amount over three times as large.

Why has three times as much energy been required to change state as to make an obvious change in temperature? The answer must lie in the added properties of the liquid and gaseous forms as contrasted with the solid. The binding of this energy results in a more complex formation and, hence, in such emergent properties of water as surface tension and solvency and kinetic energy in steam.

Our analogy suggests that developmental stages similarly bind energy which results in emergent properties. They are not mere vague areas on a smooth growth curve which shade into one another; they are as well defined and discrete as different levels of water in a flight of locks. Energy has been transformed and bound to escalate the developmental process from one level to another—just as energy is necessary to lift a canal boat in a lock—and this bound energy permits the more complex expressions, formations and emergent properties of the new stage. In short, older stages have been reorganized and reintegrated into the new form which has new emphasis and new characteristics. Their basic patterns have been superseded with new organization; it is not so much that their old order has been lost as that a new order has been emphasized. The same situation prevails in music when a theme originally played on a single orchestral instrument is *developed* so that it is now heard on a choir of different instruments in a more complex form. The theme is not lost, but it is changed through elaboration and varying emphases and sequences.

Buy why should there be developmental stages at all? Why cannot development, like growth, be one smooth accretion? The answer seems to lie in the critical aspect of energy transformations within the individual, at least in the opinion of several noted theorists. According to Erikson (Evans, 1967, p. 13) Freud's original formulation of sexual developmental stages was based on "the imagery of a transformation of energy." Sullivan (1953) based his theory of self-group interaction of "dynamisms" which he defined as "the relatively enduring patterns of energy transformations which recurrently characterize interpersonal relations." And Arieti (1967, p. 334) notes that the primary process is not so much regression in the service of the ego but "an energy accessibility and availability."

The transformation and focusing of energy is the essence of both the developmental and the creative process. It is first necessary to focus energy through attention because the amount of energy available to the individual is not enough unless it is collected and not allowed to diffuse. Through the attention of the mind, this energy is focused so that it may be transformed and induce a change of state. The areas on which attention is focused are respectively first one then another of the tripartite modes of "the world," "I" and "thou". Otherwise the available energy would be weakened and diffused if expended upon all at the same time. The analog of an automobile battery supplying a high voltage spark to the different pistons in succession comes at once to mind. This sequential aspect of focusing suggests itself at once as the reason for periodicity in developmental stage theory.

PERIODIC ASPECTS OF THE THEORY OF DEVELOPMENTAL STAGES

It is surprising how few researchers or theorists have considered periodicity as a function of human development, despite the ample opportunity for its observation both in the natural elements (the Mendeleev periodic table) and in human biology (the menstrual cycle in women). Periodicity occurs when the same pattern of events is seen to run through a higher development as has been contained in a corresponding pattern from a lower sequence. Mathematically, 1—n isomorphisms are discovered due to the influence of two overriding independent variables. In the periodic table of the elements, these are the numbers of electrons in the shells and the number of protons in the nucleus. Awareness of these variables helps us to fill spaces in such a model and hence to make predictions and draw conclusions and extrapolations. This must be done with caution because, while nature is generally orderly, it may provide some surprises since the world of experience is often more complex than man's anthropomorphic view of it. Even the periodic table reveals this in its divagations among the rare earths. While being aware of the possibility of periodicity in human development, which would point to underlying variables, attempts should not be made to fit the theory of developmental process into a Procrustean bed. Thus it is possible to speculate that since Freud's five affective developmental stages fit rather neatly the chronological ages of Piaget's five cognitive stages, and since Erikson has built four more stages out of the last Freudian (genital) stage, some future theorist may find four associated cognitive stages in adulthood—it is possible, but we should be unhappy if it does not quite match.

The goodness of fit of the Freudian (sexual libido), Eriksonian (ego strength) and Piagetian (cognitive development) theories to developmental stages is remarkable, however. When these various views are brought together synoptically, one begins to sense periodic rhythms, which reveal that the whole conceptualization of developmental stage theory is more significant than has been heretofore realized. Indeed, these stages may be divided into a tripartite grouping, depending upon the direction of the attention of the psyche, whether outward toward the world, inward toward the self or with love toward another person.

Figure 1 clearly shows the periodic nature of developmental stages, consisting of triads of stages of infancy, youth and adulthood. The horizontal triads consist in reality of three categories: the world, the ego and the other, with the third personal pronoun (it, they) characteristic of the first stage, the first personal pronoun (I) characteristic of the second, and the second personal pronoun (thou) of the third. We have dubbed the columns "latency," "identity" and "creativity," respectively, and indicated the Eriksonian and Piagetian names for the stages—taking the liberty of filling in some guesses for the cognitive aspects of the latter three stages. Thus the diagram becomes an open-ended periodic table of developmental stages which may be used as a model for testing and hypothesismaking in regard to developmental process.

Each stage has a special relationship and affinity for another three stages removed from it. Stages 1, 4, and 7 (trust, industry and generativity) are noticeable for a peculiarly thing-oriented, sexually latent aspect dealing with the relationship of the individual with his world of experience. In stage 1 it is the world of precepts; in stage 4, the size, shape, form and color of things and what one can make out of them; in stage 7, the world of significant others (such as children) who are not love objects in a libidinal sense. This may also broaden to the world of ideas, formulas, productions, art creations and other "mental children." Freud by naming the fourth stage "latency" intuitively grasped the thing-oriented, nonaffectively valent nature of this stage and its columnar family. The drop in sexual interest as the child "cools" it through the oedipal resolution entering stage 4 is particularly noticeable. He literally stops trying to "make people"

		ADULT			YOUTH			INFANT	
Class								LATENCY	IDENTITY	CREATIVITY
Pronoun								3 it, they	1 I, me	2 thou
Realm								THE WORLD	THE EGO	THE OTHER
No.		7	8	9	4	5	6	1	2	3
Erikson		GENERATIVITY	EGO-INTEGRITY	(AGAPE—LOVE)	INDUSTRY	IDENTITY	INTIMACY	TRUST	AUTONOMY	INITIATIVE
Piaget		(Psychedelic)	(Illumination)		Concrete operations	Formal operations	(Creativity)	Sensimotor	Preoperational	Intuitive
Mode					interrogative	subjunctive		none	imperative	optative
Erikson Virtues		Production—care	Renunciation—wisdom		Method—competence	Devotion—fidelity	Love—affiliation	Drive—hope	Self-control—willpower	Direction—purpose
Age		26–40 (?)	40—onward		7–12	13–17	18–25	0–1	2–3	4–6

Figure 1. Developmental Stages (After Erikson and Piaget)

in favor of making things. Not so easily spotted—because often adults have difficulty in entering the generativity period—is the sexual abatement in favor or nurturance of children or sublimation to create some innovative production which occurs with parenthood or mastery of some medium. It is as if the "name of the game" changes so that the primary attention is focused off libidinal drives to other more thing-oriented objects.

A second common aspect of the first, fourth and seventh stages is the immersion in the world of the senses. It is a practical time when things get done and changes occur. In combination with this regard for the external world, there is a certain calmness or coolness of the ego which results in a lack of self-consciousness. The infant, the boy and the parent are so busy with their activities, so completely absorbed in experiencing, that they have little time to assess their feelings or to search for their identity. After the tasks of this stage are completed, they will return to a new identity search on more advanced levels, fortified with their accomplishments in the real world.

By contrast with the previous, the second, fifth and eighth stages are ego bound, ego oriented, and ego circumscribed. They are all about "me" (my identity, my existence and interpersonal relationships and my salvation). They are times of searching introspection, of withdrawal rather than return, of defiance of authority, rather than obedience to it, and of "marching to the music of a different drum." In each of these periods man tries to come to terms with himself. In stage 2 he finds his identity or ego, in stage 5 he redefines it in terms of what he can do as a young adult, and in stage 8 he again redefines it in terms of the meaning of his life and death in the cosmos.

Parents and society often find those involved in this set of stages rather difficult to live with. Whether it is the infant's negativism, the adolescent's clamor for independence or the budding saint's march to the sea to make salt, the attitude and action of the individual is frequently anathema to authority figures, be it active resistance or passive disdain.

For the individual in these times of withdrawal, it is very easy to believe that no one understands us, that we are somehow different, unique and incongruent with the rest of humanity. We often spend too many hours in self-examination, either in reproach or adulation with "the world forgotten and by the world forgot." If the world is "too much with us" in stages 1, 4 and 7, it is too little with us ofttimes in stages 2, 5 and 8, for we are busy examining our own navels. One consequence of this overemphasis on introspection is a kind of moodiness which results from the discrepancy between what the ego wants itself to be and what it finds it can be and do.

Stages 3 and 6 (initiative and intimacy) deal with the love relationship and its expansion from narcissistic self-love through oedipal love of parents to generalized heterosexual love, to fixation on some individual person. (For all we know there may exist stage 9, where agape love, in the manner of a Buddha or Messiah embraces all mankind.) Since love is requisite for creation on a mental as well as a physical plane, it is not surprising that stages 3 and 6 have special interest for us as students of creativity. We have already described in chapter 1 how creativity first develops in the initiative stage from the control over the environment experienced through the affectional approach of the opposite-sexed parent. A similar feeling occurs in the sixth stage (intimacy), when adolescent creativity is normally enhanced through the inspiration of the opposite-sexed beloved figure. In the latter instance, however, biological consummation can in some cases reduce the high energy potential aroused so that it is more often when this consummation is delayed, or prevented at least in part, that we get great art, music and literature. Obviously this kind of situation differs with different individuals, some of whom (like Elizabeth Barrett Browning) find fulfillment in love and block in the frustration of it.

In consequence of the connection between love in our lives and creativity, if we want to become creative, we should put more love into our lives. Most of us live on a starvation diet so far as love is concerned. What man could not create if he were universally admired, valued and inspired? This principle is not to imply that sexual freedom or promiscuity is a prerequisite for creative action, but it does suggest that more openness and demonstrativeness in love and affection in all our social relationships, more awareness of our feeling aspects and less inhibition of them might open up doors now closed by custom.

Barron (1968) reports that creative persons find other ways to deal with impulse than suppressing it. Who has not found inspiration in the unexpected valuing of himself by another? Indeed, this phenomenon and the power release that accompanies it is one of the great sources of energy in group therapy sessions or in Rogerian basic encounter groups.

In saying that stages 3 and 6 are those in which the I-thou relationships and creativity are particularly emphasized, I do not mean to imply that creativity is completely absent at other stages of development. It is just that the developmental process naturally emphasizes these factors at these times. Love and hence creativity may enter our lives environmentally at any time, and to the degree that one is found in abundance the other is likely to be present. In these instances, something personal has occurred—some vivid experience or significant relationship not predicated in the developmental sequence—and it is this personal good fortune, rather than the developmental syndrome, which has released creative power.

If latency stages 1, 4 and 7 may be described as "cool" and the identity stages of 2, 5 and 8 are introspective, then stages 3 and 6 may best be characterized as loving, spontaneous and joyful. Here affectional impulses are at their height; here one gives the identity one has just discovered to another; here the world and the self become fused in the wonder of the beloved—the up phase when all goes well and one is comfortable and sure of one's beloved results in great happiness. But when one is alone, and things are scary, without one's beloved (who may be paying too much attention to a younger sibling or a rival lover), then one is consumed with jealousy and lives in the depths of despair.

The key question of both the third and sixth stages is, "Am I in control of my environment through the aegis of my beloved or is my environment in control of me?" Developmental tasks of different periods have a different flavor, however, even if they refer to the same basic issue. The possessive jealous oedipal love of a son for his mother in the third stage is different from the heterosexual genital intimacy of a young man in the sixth stage. Both of these stages give creativity an extra impetus, but the two kinds of creativity have different flavors and characteristics. This fact has led many researchers to note that the child's creativity is not the same as the creative production of young adults. The creativity of the third (initiative) stage is exhibitionistic, dramatic, often repetitive and generally fragmentary. The creativity of a young adult is characterized by more unity, coherence, daring and brilliance. It is truly novel, and often displays scope, mastery and vigor. Whether the one develops into the other depends, of course, on environmental conditions. A good start helps the growing child to a more open style of life. Environmental deprivation, however, may force him to become destructive or hostile or fall by the wayside. Even too much success in the initiative period may give his creativity a "kooky" turn which does not allow him to integrate it into future development or come to grips with the disciplinary skills of the industry period.

Another youth may blossom in late adolescence without the benefits of narcissistic creativity because, having learned his basic skills and formal operations well, he has somehow been able to break through into the creative ground. Longitudinal research may eventually show that form prevails in general and that a good start in the third stage is the best assurance of another successful round in the sixth stage. Incidentally, this kind of longitudinal follow-up is badly needed research. One becomes creative as a by-product of the inspiration of the beloved. One strives to please, and in pleasing the loved one, pulls things out of the preconscious that one hardly knew were there. Or alternatively, because one's mental health is improved, one finds the preconscious teeming with treasure to share with the beloved, and these goodies often bubble forth without conscious effort.

Whatever has potential for creativity has potential for destructivity also. Vishnu and Shiva are but different aspects of Brahma. We do not find it surprising that the young child creates and destroys practically in the same breath. For some reason, however, we are surprised that university students, deep in the intimacy period, who are denied their creative outlets through stereotyped teaching of obsolete curriculum and authoritarianism, turn to destructiveness in trying to express themselves. Our Puritan ethic of inhibition is also offended when the same youth demonstrate the more undiscriminating and public forms of love and affection. Perhaps we would do better to ask if there is a message for us in this unacceptable behavior and to consider what we might do to make higher education more innovative and more humane.

Just as one finds in the horizontal variable in the Mendeleev periodic table of the elements a basic explication of nature in the number of electrons in the outer shell, so one would expect to find similar basic properties in the column headings of our periodic table of developmental process. It is evident from several sources that this is so. What has been disclosed here depends, however, on one's frame of reference. A semanticist or grammarian would note that we are dealing with the personal pronouns: first person, the self; second person, the other; third person, the world. A religiously oriented individual, noting that our column heads can be described as ego-presence, creative-love and thing-latency would naturally think of the Trinity: Father, Son and Holy Ghost. From a psychological point of view, it is not so much that these theological terms are valid as that they represent an early attempt, necessarily clothed in religious language, to approximate three fundamental aspects through which man's mind apprehends reality. The three developmental thrusts are continuous but with different emphases recurring periodically in elaborated and elevated forms.

OPEN-ENDED PERIODIC TABLE OF DEVELOPMENT AND ITS IMPLICATIONS

One of the consequences of setting the Mendeleev table up in periodic form was that it was left open ended with blank spaces for elements not discovered at the time of its publication. Mendeleev, indeed, predicted the existence of helium, then undiscovered. Spaces for other heavier atoms were left blank until filled in by the results of discoveries in radioactivity and atomic research. It is evident that an open-ended model is most fruitful in being able to accommodate without modification new discoveries in science. It is indeed heuristic in the best sense of the word.

Setting up the developmental stages in periodic style immediately confronts us with a similar fascinating problem in open endedness. Are there rarer or as yet unknown stages of cognitive development to go with the already found Eriksonian stages? Are there advanced affective stages which have rarely if ever been observed in any human? How do such putative stages fit the literature of creativity, psychedelia and illumination? We enter here on speculation early developed by Bucke (1929) in *Cosmic Consciousness*, but further discussion of these possibilities will have to be deferred until chapter 7.

Before leaving this matter, however, it should be noted that periodicity is a method employed often to secure the occurrence of a function whose continual operation would place too much tax on the energies of the individual. The breeding season or rut in animals is a good example. By this means a sequence of process is devised, which allows for the orderly discharge of activities which could not take place continuously.

When traffic flowing smoothly and constantly along two intersecting highways reaches an intersection at a grade, some change has to take place. A traffic light permits the flow of traffic first on one road and then on the other. This cycle is necessary not only at a highway junction but wherever full communication flow would overload a given station.

It is so with man, especially with regard to those functions which would either require too much expenditure of energy or which are emergent in the sense that they are grasped only by superior individuals for a short time when they are in top mental health. Because man cannot apprehend all aspects of reality at once, reality has to be ordered by man into a cyclic or periodic succession of partial views. Thus in physics we get the wave and the corpuscular theory of light. We find the mind alternatively using cognitive and affective means to sense the world. The periodic aspects of developmental stage theory appear necessary for similar reasons.

CHARACTERISTIC TASKS AND STRENGTHS

The changing emphases of developmental stages may be compared to the performance of flamenco dancers. All the dancers are on stage throughout the performance, yet each holds the spotlight at different times as he "does his stuff," to the applause of the others who form the chorus. So it is with developmental process: each aspect is always present, but each different characteristic comes front and center at its appropriate time and is emphasized while the others act as a kind of background chorus.

Thus these stages can be regarded as the stations of the cross or the labors of Hercules, each designed to impart a different aspect of grace or valor of the developing individual. Like the ordeals of a candidate for knighthood or the vigils of a novitiate for a monastery, each act differentiates a certain quality and, when accomplished, contributes this particular strength to the whole personality. As each new task is successfully resolved, a new strength is incorporated into the individual; consequently the person becomes many faceted and capable of interchanges between existing qualities and new powers (such as a telephone switchboard can connect new subscribers to the generality in a developing suburb). If a task is not well performed, a certain characteristic weakness remains. Missing basic mathematical skills in the third grade may leave one ever reluctant to balance one's checkbook.

Even humor often reveals our sense of the importance of developmental tasks and the consequent embarrassment of failures at them. For example, walking, talking and toilet training are major tasks of the second (autonomy) period. Uneasiness about and half-remembered struggle for success in these tasks give point to jokes about someone slipping on a banana peel, stuttering or having a bladder accident.

Each stage is powered by the individual's drive for mastery in tasks appropriate to the stage. Thus in the fourth period (industry) the child has an innate drive to master the alphanumeric system, to build and manipulate tool objects, etc. The available energy of the individual is focused toward accomplishing the critical tasks of the period. When this is not accomplished, there must be powerful inhibitors in the individual himself (such as the accumulation of previous failures) or from the cultural mores, which may interfere by imposing tasks which are irrelevant (such as enforced military service) or contrary to the essential thrust of developmental progress. To succeed at the tasks of a particular stage produces mental health; to fail them or be thwarted in attempting them is apt to produce mental illness or at best hostility and other negative emotions. Often destructiveness and delinquency in youth may be related to this cultural cause.

Not all failures are culturally induced, however. An individual may avoid attending to or may ignore the characteristic tasks of the stage he should be in by rehearsing or repeating his success (or lack of it) in the tasks of the previous level. Thus lonely young adolescents expend all their energy on school achievement, while immature young men shy away from heterosexual intimacy to continue their search for an identity. Equally often, adults in the generativity period play hide-and-seek games instead of turning their interests toward the nurturance of children or innovative production, while matrons of fifty are still child and grandchild oriented instead of becoming altruistic long after their children have outgrown and rejected them.

A similar lag is seen in the repetition of cognitive tasks one stage below developmental level. Thus those in the sixth stage (intimacy) will frequently be satisfied with formal operations (convergent production) rather than risk divergent thinking and creativity. Moodiness may be a sign that the ego is having trouble with the present task, and boredom may indicate that the individual would like to return and toy with simpler tasks of a previous stage.

DIFFERENTIAL DEVELOPMENT

Human development is orderly and sequential in that measurements within a developmental area on different individuals vary less than the mean difference between developmental stages. This statement by no means requires that these individual differences become null; hence differential developmental patterns do exist (there is "wobble" in the track), and differential developmental rates can be found. We could restate this last point by saying that although we customarily use chronological age as the independent variable in developmental analysis, organismic age would be a more exact substitution. Piaget conceded that his stages were "only approximate" chronologically and could perhaps be accelerated or delayed by environmental stimulation or deficit.

The implications of differential development cannot be fully analyzed here, but it may be instructive to give some examples of it. The first example chosen has to do with a comparison of maturity in the gifted and average adolescent.

In comparison with the average adolescent who soon starts an active sex life, the gifted adolescent (who usually matures physically earlier) goes through a kind of latency period in which heterosexual expression may be inhibited for several years. Kinsey and his colleagues (1948) indeed found striking differences between boys of different classes in this regard, and reported that when a boy from a low socioeconomic background was upwardly mobile, his sex habits from the earliest times he could remember were those of the class into which he was going to migrate.

Adolescent sexual latency in the superior individual is a further example of the "Foetalization of the Ape" hypothesis, as we have extended it, in that the superior individual is allowed to "stretch out" these developmental stages. It is also an example of "feminization" (which we shall discuss in chapter 6) to enable the individual to resist the biological aging, and secure a larger percentage of the life span spent in the more creative phases.

As seen in figure 2, the gifted adolescent is both more mature and less mature than the average adolescent. He is more mature when compared directly with his age mate. He is less mature, however, when the ratio between his present and potential maturity is compared with the ratio between the average adolescent's present and potential maturity. In short, there is more of him left to grow.

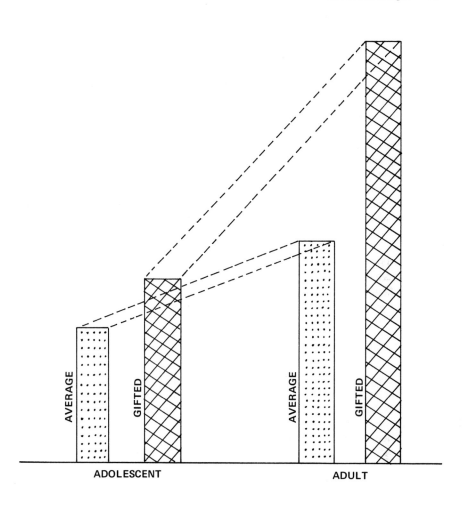

Figure 2. Gifted Adolescent

There is a hierarchy of the degree of prehension the individual holds on different factors of the intellect. Cognition-memory of units and classes are much more strongly held and for longer periods than, for example, divergent production and evaluation of semantic implications. Under stress, alcohol, fatigue, psychosis and the like, the higher functioning is lost in a selective order, retaining verbalization to the last. Hence some higher abilities such as creativity and other exotic aspects of intellect may appear tenuously and only spasmodically in individuals at their most propitious times of health or development and may be lost with the onset of senility, fatigue, disease or other untoward cause. This kind of operation also contributes to the effect of differential development.

Another example of differential development concerns the availability of energy for escalating developmental process from one level to the next. To produce this development, energy must be fed into the system. This is as true of individual development as it is of the latent heat of fusion or the excitation of electrons to higher orbits. This energy requirement results in some degree of strain at the jump points. There may not be enough energy available for both growth and adjustment at the same time. Perhaps the child, retooling mentally from the concrete-operations to the formal-operations period will suffer a shortage of available energy in the process, and this will be reflected as Torrance (1964) demonstrated as a creativity slump around the fourth grade.

SUMMARY

The central thesis of this chapter revolves around the transformation or refocus of energy in developmental stages. The need for energy focusing and shifts in attention lead to periodicity in developmental stages which have important consequences. This model produces a synoptic fusion of Eriksonian and Piagetian stages arranged in periodic three-cycle fashion in which the individual's concern with the world, I and thou, reoccurs at three levels of maturity. Each stage has characteristic properties. Important for our purposes among these properties are the creative aspects of stage 3 (initiative) and stage 6 (intimacy). Guesses are hazarded concerning higher cognitive stages to fit the affective stages named by Erikson. Finally there is comment and example of development in differential form at various levels.

Implied but not yet clarified are certain aspects of stage development which we have named escalation. These aspects will be analyzed in chapter 3.

3

ESCALATION

I do not wish to represent man as he is, but only as he might be.

—Paul Klee

The construct of escalation is helpful in understanding the process of development. "Escalate," a recently coined word, means to raise the level of action *by discrete jumps*; it derives from moving up an escalator, a flight of stairs or a ladder. When one shifts gears in an automobile, one escalates; this is not just a matter of going faster—more properly, one engages a different service of power.

Escalation is used in this chapter as a concept embracing five different although interrelated aspects of development: succession, discontinuity, emergence, differentiation and integration. Each of these characteristics defines a different facet of escalation, and these will then be used to analyze concept formation in the developing child and the interrelations between cognitive and affective developmental systems in producing mental health and the possibility of creativity. (The cognitive system refers to the rational development of the mind and is covered by Piagetian developmental stages; the affective system covers emotional development and is covered by Eriksonian developmental stages.) The components of escalation are summarized in figure 3.

COMPONENT	DESCRIPTION	PIAGET'S NEAREST TERM	RELEVANT MATERIAL
Succession	A fixed order of hierarchical stages	Hierarchicization	Decalages (cultural and personal lags)
Discontinuity	A discrete succession of discontinuous equilibration	Equilibration	Each stage has characteristic properties and tasks
Emergence	The budding and making of the implicit, explicit	Consolidation	Budding
Differentiation	Fixation and shift in emphasis	Integration	Fixation Metamorphosis
Integration	A Gestalt of structures d'ensemble	Structuring	Summation structures d'ensemble (parts which assemble to make a whole)

Figure 3. The Components of Escalation

SUCCESSION

The term "succession" implies that there is a fixed order or hierarchy among developmental processes. The ordered hierarchy in turn implies a continual rise in the level of action at each stage. The order is invariant, although the time sequence is organismic and not strictly chronological. Piaget (Pinard and Laurendeau, 1969, p. 125) calls this property *hierarchicization*, an accurate although awkwardly translated term, and points out that this attribute at once leads to the concept of *decalages* (or developmental lags) which depend on personal and cultural idiosyncrasies.

The concept of succession implies that the track of development is fixed, in that a given stage follows and never precedes another. The rate of succession through stages and the extent of development at any stage, however, is flexible since these are influenced by the nature of the organism and its environment. Man likes to think of himself as a free animal wandering over a large range, able to go wherever he wishes and to do whatever he likes. By discovering that we cannot do what we please, we find that modern research suggests that this model is not appropriate to the facts. A better example would be that of a powerful locomotive set firmly on the tracks with few possibilities of switching to other lines. Speed and destination are dependent upon the engineer's decisions and the available fuel. The main degree of freedom lies in his ability to accelerate or slow down the speed with which the engine goes down the track.

DISCONTINUITY

The concept of discontinuity parallels that of succession. One cannot imagine a flight of locks in a canal as other than a succession of discontinuities, each with the water level at equilibrium. The order is invariant. One could not have the first lock, then the fifth, then the fourth, third and second. As a flight of locks contains water at various stages of equilibrium whereas a waterfall does not, so this discontinuity of ordered sequences allows for equilibrium at various stages as a smooth growth curve does not. The term applied by Piaget (Pinard and Laurendeau, 1969, p. 145) to this phenomenon is *equilibration* (an ordered succession of differing levels of equilibrium).

The concept of discontinuity implies that there is available an additional input of energy to escalate development from one level to the next. This extra increment, as indicated in chapter 2, is similar to the latent heat of fusion in that it is necessary to transform the state and properties of the operand. Just as shifting an automobile into higher gear allows for more efficient use of available power, additional energy is transformed to the freer properties of a new and higher state. Any teacher who has observed a child emerge as an adolescent through the process of sexual maturation has recognized the vast increase in intellectual power and scope wrought by the developmental change. New and complex motivational patterns may also appear as outcomes of this discontinuity.

EMERGENCE

Emergence, or the debut of new powers, is the third aspect of escalation. As the child progresses from one stage to another in the developmental sequence, qualities which were implicit or covert in a previous stage become explicit or overt in the next or following stage. This bringing out or manifestation of emergent characteristics, some of them unexpected or unrecognized at the earlier level, is seen in many phases of development as the budding or preparation for the next phase.

Each phase contains not only the full explication of qualities which were inchoate previously, but also a prototype bud or other preliminary indication of those which will later become manifest. An example is the intuitive conservation of volume perceived by the child in the third stage (initiative) versus the actual conservation of volume during the fourth (industry) stage. As Piaget observes, the child in the earlier stage will often be able to conserve volume but cannot tell you why, whereas later he can do both. Piaget calls this attribute "consolidation" (Pinard and Laurendeau, 1969, p. 129), in that a given stage is simultaneously a summation of the accomplishments of the previous stages and a preparation for the tasks of the next stage.

The elaboration of an attribute that previously had been only a trace is more than just the cognitive spelling out of an intuition. The explication denotes permanency in development. Earlier, the promised attribute is a "sometime thing," now appearing, now disappearing. For it is a rule in developmental sequence that powers are possessed in a hierarchical order—first, in tenuous form or only at intervals; later on, to be more permanently apprehended. As when a friend comes to visit us, he calls us first on the phone, and we have cognition of him through one sensory channel; we think of him off and on. Soon he arrives in the flesh, and we experience him fully through all sensory channels at once. The Portuguese proverb distinguishes "A trace, a path, a lane, and a highway"; and in a similar manner do we—spasmodically, intuitively, iconically and finally symbolically—apprehend new concepts.

Bruner's sequence of enactive, iconic and symbolic representation of experience hence constitutes an example of emergence (1966, p. 11). What has been a trace at one time becomes more clearly a path at the next level, a lane at the succeeding and a highway at last.

This process of escalation could not occur if there were not at every stage the preparatory process we call "budding." Budding refers to the implicit appearance at every early stage of the growth potential of the succeeding stages. At each stage, development not only unfolds and differentiates the characteristic properties of that stage, but it displays in bud form the epigenesis of the next stage. This aspect of escalation cannot be explained by the history of the individual but by inherent developmental tendencies of the species. It seems ludicrous that the four-year-old boy will form an oedipal attachment toward his mother, but this prepares him, much later in the intimacy stage, for a true genital approach to the beloved person of the opposite sex.

Erikson (Evans, 1967, p. 21) suggests that the rudiments of character emerge in the autonomy stage and "develop further in each stage as shown on my epigenetic diagram. . . . They become more complex and differentiated, and therefore undergo renewed crises."[1] Erikson used the word "epigenetic" to mean "upon emergence" in very much the same way that we have employed "escalation" to signify that one item develops on the shoulders of another. Erikson later remarks (Evans, 1967, pp. 40–41) about the one-stage-after-another approach: "It misses the nature of epigenetic stages in which each stage adds something specific to all later ones, and makes an ensemble out of all earlier ones."

DIFFERENTIATION

Differentiation refers to the escalatory attribute which clarifies, "fixates" and modifies the emphasis in developmental processes. It resolves or fixates in the sense that "focusing in" on an object by a zoom camera lens clarifies the optical field. Perhaps due to translational difficulties, Piaget (Pinard and Laurendeau, 1969, p. 124) does not find a word which exactly fits this definition. The nearest is "integration" by which he means restructuring and coordination, which would be much like our change of emphasis. Differentiation, however, has been well delineated by Bower and Hollister (1968), and its contribution to concept formation receives fuller treatment in "Concept Formation and Conceptualization" of this chapter.

Fixation as an Aspect of Developmental Processes

Developmental processes which are loose and inchoate at early stages tend to become bound, defined and fixated at higher stages. The increase in specialism and specificity results in part from the accumulation of habits and conditioned responses. Fixation is more complex, however, than mere conditioning; it involves selection of tempos, pacing, and the development of likes and dislikes of objects and processes. Experiences become organized into value systems which determine choice into similar patterns. A girl at the heterosexual stage of development will be attracted to boys in general; later she will love a particular boy. Fixation not only means that the attribute will be held more tightly, but that it will be apprehended in the same manner each time. The habituation of response tends to put an end to creative play variations on that response; we learn to do something well in a certain way, and it becomes more certain that we will do it in that way without variation. The process is analogous to "type casting" in the theater.

Differentiation as a Shift of Emphasis on Metamorphosis

A striking aspect of developmental sequence is the sudden switch in emphasis from one stage to another. Almost without warning between stage three

---

[1]From page 21, Evans, R. I. *Dialog with Erik Erikson*, Copyright 1967, Harper & Row Publishers. Used by permission.

(initiative) and stage four (industry) the six-year-old child stops valuing his behavior in terms of bad and good, love and hate, reflecting strong affection for his parents, and literally "cools it" by beginning to start making things instead of "making people."

Of a sudden, everything you have said to your child becomes as the blowing wind; he has simply left you and fallen under the evil influence of a neighbor's child. What this young monster says and does is gospel indeed. They wear the same clothes, eat the same breakfast cereal, watch the same TV shows, have secrets from you, and all at once your love and affection is displaced by hobbies, crafts, tree houses, secret clubs, a gang of boys, no display of affection and a general cool outlook toward the world which looks at facts instead of feelings. And he continually pesters you with "who," "where," "what," "when" and "why."

A similar switch of emphasis faces the parent of a teenager who seems to have outgrown the family and regards himself or herself as an unwilling hostage in prison with only a telephone as a lifeline to his agemates. These metamorphoses, while traumatic for parents, are necessary crises in the escalation of development from one stage to another. Were it not for the stress and strain of adolescence, growth would result not in an adult but simply in a monster-sized child. To become an adult, the reorganization and reemphasis of previous habits, attitudes and values are essential.

The problems of differentiation are compounded by the fact that it is by no means certain that early success will help and forward individual developmental escalation. To be sure, failure will not; but too much success at a stage can result in fixation at the stage. Escalation is not simply accretion or more of the same thing; it is a metamorphosis which amounts to a new and different ball game. Often those most successful in one phase will wish to remain there, replaying their successes and refusing to get on with the tasks of the next stage.

An individual who has been only moderately successful in earlier stages can blossom out in a later stage. This is usually because he finds himself and gets personal "hang ups" straightened out. Change of emphasis insures a greater degree of freedom in the developmental pattern, therefore, since the race is not always toward the shift. The process of development is itself therapeutic, and so long as the thrust of development continues, there is also the possibility of self-actualization as well as the probability of improvement.

INTEGRATION

Integration, the final attribute of escalation, synthesizes the others. It is in some respects the mathematical integral of the previous aspects. A mathematical integral of an algebraic function is a related function of the next higher degree with the addition of a constant which must be determined by observation, thus giving two sources of extra freedom and one of greater complexity. It is not surprising that a higher synthesis, greater complexity and new degrees of freedom are characteristic properties of the concept of integration.

Piaget (Pinard and Laurendeau, 1969, pp. 129—136) describes an attribute called integration, but fitting our scheme better is his term "structuring." The tasks of a stage are not simple accretions of the previous stages, but are interconnected to form a meaningful unit (like the rafters of a roof) which unites into a gestalt called by Piaget *"structures d'ensemble."* This is more characteristic of our concept than his "integration" which simply refers to reemphasis. Following are some familiar examples of integration:

(1)   The child's interest in various parts of his body seen during stage two (autonomy) now becomes integrated in stage three (initiative) into a narcissistic love of his whole body. The energy of the parts becomes bound into energy for the whole.

(2)   In the transformation from child to adolescent, there is increase in complexity of emotion, and such emergent qualities as genital sexual drives, greater capacity for tenderness and feeling and more intellectual range, all of which form a newer synthesis of previously identified aspects and permit new degrees of freedom and choice.

(3)   The enhanced ego concept of the third stage (initiative) over previous stages is an illustration of increased complexity. The earlier simple assertion of "me-ness" now takes on a new quality in terms of what "me" can do. (I am the person who can coordinate my body: I am so delightfully winsome that everyone will love me, pay attention to me and revolve their lives around me.) The production of emergent qualities is illustrated by that of creative fantasy in the four year old. Responding to the warm affect of the opposite-sexed parent, the child now dips deeper and deeper into the preconscious to produce creative products to show off to this charming adult with whom he is having his first love affair. The valence of the budding "I-thou" relationship is indeed something new.

Integration also embraces a higher synthesis of already delineated elements; hence it summates the concept of escalation. Who among us has not felt the thrill of driving a geared car on an open road and shifting into overdrive as the highway clears ahead? The car goes faster with less effort, because the gear ratio has been changed and the engine labors less per mile per hour traveled. We can do this and experience the consequent sense of freedom and elation at high speeds only on an excellent road. We feel this way even though there is no more potential power in the auto than there was at rest or backing up a steep grade. We are in a sense self-actualizing the automobile for we are using it at its utmost at the task for which it was built. This top efficiency at any stage of development is reached only through a harmonious psychic-biologic relationship resulting from excellent mental health on the part of the individual which enables him to integrate his total potential or, as we say in current slang, to "put it all together."

CONCEPT FORMATION AND CONCEPTUALIZATION

Having now completed the definition of five aspects of escalation: succession, discontinuity, emergence, differentiation and integration, let us see how they apply to some of the major processes of development. The first example will be a discussion of their utility in an analysis of concept formation.

Bucke (1929) postulated that there were three types of consciousness: (a) simple consciousness such as that possessed by the higher animals; (b) self-consciousness such as that possessed by the average rational man; and (c) cosmic consciousness, possessed rarely and spasmodically by few members of the human race. Leaving out the more contentious part of his argument, most people would agree that at least one difference between men and animals is the possession of self-consciousness. While present in every normal adult, it is by no means present in the child at birth, but seems to dawn as part of the ego in the second (autonomy) stage, increasing through childhood to effloresce in the fifth (identity) stage. It is certainly not coincidental that the same period is identified by Piaget for the beginning of the ability to conceptualize. Conceptualization starts when the child can decenter and flowers in formal operations when the youth can reason and deal with cause and effect through hypothesis making.

The chief cognitive method of concept formation involves the ability to form an intellectually negotiable concept, more or less isomorphic to external experience out of a series of encounters with that experience each of which is consensually validated through contact with others. It involves skills of cognition, memory, convergent and divergent production, and evaluation—in short the operational abilities of the Guilford "Structure of Intellect."

Bruner (1966) has brilliantly discussed enactive, iconic and symbolic representation, three prominent ways in which the child develops these skills. In Sullivan's theory (1953, p. xiv) the conceptualization of experience occurs in three modes which he called "prototaxic, parataxic and syntaxic." The crucial role of language in human experience is pointed up by the demarcation between the modes. Experience occurring before symbolization is referred to as prototaxic, private symbols designate parataxic, and syntaxic is used for experience which can be communicated by means of symbols. Sullivan's phrase for this was "consensual validation," and he saw this confirmation of our experience by others, when we are able intellectually to negotiate it, as a great help in reducing the anxiety of the ego in removing experience from the uncanny "not-me" category to that of everyday occurrence.

As each of us tries to make sense out of our conceptualization of the "big, blooming, buzzing confusion" of the external world, we attempt to bring more and more of it within the explanation of rationality, first in that our precepts are perceived by others and second in that our concepts are conceived by others. The concept model will be an aid to our thinking only if it is a viable strategy in the Bruner sense; that is, is it isomorphic with the real world?

Kelly (1955) postulated that our perceptions of the world of experience are constrained by the way in which we anticipate events. Is our experience of the world constrained by the way in which we conceptualize it? Some schools of thought believe that the way we conceptualize data governs our selected attention to it, and hence the pattern and meaning of the data is controlled by our conceptualization and is not anterior to it. Since it is data plus meaning which we perceive and conceptualize, it is meaningless for us to talk about the existence of nature before becoming conscious of it, for there is no meaning for us, and hence no semantic reality to nature prior to our conceptualization of it, any more than there is an absolute motion of pure ether. What we call "data" of nature has already been conceptualized or we could not know it. This is why mind cannot accept the possibility of total meaninglessness of the universe.

Following this line of reasoning, we find that the world of nature cannot be described as a discrete series of events independent of any observer, for the only reality we can know lies in our conceptualization of nature not whatever may be before that. The meaning and hence the reality is in the sometimes different, but generally similar, perceptions of events by different observers, each conceptualizing in his own way. Minds oriented to conceptualize in one way will tend to see similar events; minds oriented in another manner will conceptualize differently and hence will report somewhat different events in a somewhat different order in a kind of social relativity. Each is relatively true because it is relatively meaningful. While our language appears to invest reality in natural forms and not in the transactional relationships in our minds (wherein the true meaning lies), there is no final reality or meaning in nature independent of the consciousness which conceptualizes it. Conceptualization, therefore, is not an artifact of culture; it is a necessary condition of being alive and conscious.

Conceptualization involves the use of models and their use is significant not so much because the model is "true" as because it helps us to organize large and complex areas of experience and to predict outcomes. Better that the model be heuristic, leading to useful outcomes, than that it be true, leading to a complete representation of reality. For example, Piaget's logical model of conservation of numbers, involving closure, associativity, identity and inversion may not be explicitly understood by the child, any more than he understands the grammatical structure of English. The model is a useful construct in analyzing behavior because it fits in with other cognitive structures familiar to us and enables us to predict results with some accuracy.

This reasoning brings us close to the classical philosophical argument between the Nominalists and the Realists—the former arguing that reality resides in our structuring of the world and the latter, that there is an independent reality. One of the most reassuring aspects of Piaget's theories is that he takes the middle position of interactionism in attempting a synthesis. There is a relationship between the knower and the known, each affecting the other, so that it is not just the way the environment is conceptualized by the child, it is also his developmental level which affects the reality he perceives and organizes. Hence reality for the child is relative, for he perceives it differently from reality for the adult.

The tremendous contributions of Piaget toward understanding concept formation are related to his assimilation-accommodation model. These as Flavell (1963, p. 44) points out are the two interrelated components of adaptation which together with organization makes up biological functioning.

Flavell reminds us (1963, p. 411) that Piaget revealed concept development to be a process of extraordinary and unsuspected richness. He adds:

> It is to Piaget's credit that he found a way to build so much continuity into so manifestly a stage theory of development. He did it, of course, by the simple expedient of associating the continuity with the functional aspects and the discontinuity with the structural ones.[1]

Piaget's theories constitute a "roomy" model which affords hypothesis for future research. According to Flavell (1963, p. 417), some of the face-valid measures of cognitive performance over time may result in better and more accurate mental measurements; such tests may prove more predictive of "creative, inventive or innovative capacities."

Indeed, as Flavell concludes (1963, p. 420):

> Intellectual development may be conceived as a kind of Toynbeean challenge-response affair; at selected points in his development, the society thrusts the child into new roles and different sets of cognitive demands; the child responds to this challenge by acquiring the new cognitive structures to cope with these demands.[2]

Piaget's challenge and response view of development is echoed by Bruner (1959, p. 369):

> Logical structures develop to support the new forms of commerce with the world. It is just as plainly the case that the preoperational child, protected by his parents, need not manipulate the world of objects unassisted until the pressure of independence is placed upon him, at which time concrete operations emerge. So the concretely operational child need not manipulate the world of potentiality save on the fantasy level until pressure is placed upon him at which point propositionalism begins to mark his thinking.

This concept of constant interaction between environmental stimulation and concept development is easily understood in relation to sports and physical education. No one would expect an Olympic skier or a mountain climber such as Hillary to develop without any training or mountaineering experience. Conversely, an athletic coach, trying to develop such superior athletes, would seek those boys who at an early age had superior physiques. He would then subject them to rigorous training, with frequent testing, and as much success experience as possible, enabling them to progress from one stage of competence to another until eventually they became of international competitive caliber.

Societies concerned with cognitive competence may need to reconsider the degree of environmental stimulation and early success experiences provided by their national institutions in the light of what Piaget said about the development of concept formation. Will the boy, for example, who is facile with concrete operations at eight (and hence judged to be intelligent), develop into the young man

---

[1] From page 411, Flavell, J. H. *The Developmental Psychology of Jean Piaget*, Copyright, 1963, Litton Educational Publishing Co. Used by permission.

[2] From page 420, Flavell, J. H. *The Developmental Psychology of Jean Piaget*, Copyright, 1963, Litton Educational Publishing Co. Used by permission.

who is equally facile with formal operations or creativity at twenty? What kinds of educational stimulation are most likely to ensure this escalation?

It is all very well to talk about the child's cognitive development through concrete and formal operations to creative functioning, but the child must have something to escalate. To operate, much less be creative, in the symbolic or semantic contents area, the child must master linguistics. In creating, the child gives conceptual order to his experience. Hence the proper organization of matter and material in the prior concrete operations stage is a necessary percursor of verbal creativity.

Order grows out of grouping constructs of semantic contents and then connecting them in meaningful ways. Part of this is categorizing or fitting units into appropriate classes. The diagram:

	color	
red	yellow	blue

is such a construct. Here the parameter color takes on discrete values or attributes, each of which is related to the parameter as a child is to its parent or a unit to its class, and each of which has a coeval relationship with its fellow colors. Sampson (1965) and Upton and Sampson (1961) have analyzed this process, which involves the developing use by the child of words and symbols in reification, qualification, classification, operations, analogy and structure analysis. This process is the central tie in concrete operations for it builds an isomorphism between the mental world of the child and the physical world outside. It is necessary before formal operations or creativity can begin. It is, therefore, a part of escalation of cognitive development.

Moreover, the child's cognitive escalation is tied to the modes of grammar. A glance at the following chart will be helpful:

Developmental stage	**Verbal mode**
Trust or sensimotor period	*No speech*
Autonomy or preoperational period	*Imperative mode*
Initiative or intuitive period	*Optative mode*
Industry or concrete operations period	*Interrogative mode*
Identity or formal operations period	*Subjunctive mode*

When speech arrives, the young child starts the second period with a blunt expression of nascent will—the imperative—but soon finds that the world is not quick to obey his commands. He subsides gradually into the wishful optative "I wish it were . . ." or "Would that I could .,. .," and thus fuels the fantasy of the third period. But this intuitive fantasy is soon displaced by the more matter-of-fact questioning, "who," "where," "what," "when," "why" of the interrogative mode during the fourth or concrete operations period. Later, around adolescence, the child escapes the tyranny of the fact by discovering the subjunctive mode and the power of hypothesis making through "if-then" relationships during the formal operations of the fifth developmental stage.

SUMMARY

Development involves escalation; that is, the emergence of a higher and more complex form of organization and synthesis. Just as a musical motif is developed through escalation into more complex choirs and modes, so the child's developing mind in its journey from egocentricity to altruism escalates into forms more complicated and isomorphic with reality. Greater freedom and more possibilities of creative function are therefore open. The concrete-operational child is tied to the tyranny of the interrogative mode—the reality of what actually is. The formal-operational child escapes into the freedom of contingency; he discovers the subjunctive and is thus free to become creative in "if-then" hypothesis making.

A corollary of escalation is that each stage contains the bud or implicit statement of the next stage, and each stage represents an integration or higher resolution of the previous stage. The concept of an equilibrium of discontinuities, or hierarchy of order, which never varies is also implied in the concept of escalation.

This view of developmental stages stresses the interaction of cognitive development with corresponding phases in the affective domain. As Flavell remarks: "Piaget's analysis both complements and significantly adds to Erikson's account" and "A sense of the whole child emerges more clearly in a stereoscopic integration of the two" (1963, p. 414). Indeed, the developing child progresses as on a dual staircase, one foot on the affective and the other on the cognitive risers.

Piaget and Erikson have named the staircases, and in their remarkably corresponding stages have indicated coeval stories. Within each story there are many risers (which Piaget has detailed more carefully than Erikson), and the child almost alternately makes his climb by putting first one foot on an affective and the other on a cognitive advance. The interactional balance of thought and feeling between these results in positive mental health for the whole organism. If a series of risers is missing on one staircase, the child is effectively blocked from advancing farther on either, and we say he is arrested (emotionally) or an underachiever (cognitively). The interaction is reciprocal: emotional difficulties underlie school failure; lack of cognitive competence may create a poor self concept and disrupt relations with others. The dual model has many aspects of strength not possessed by either alone, just as a study of electricity is reinforced by a simultaneous investigation of magnetism.

While Decarie (1965) has attempted to connect Piaget and Freud in developmental process, the book which best centers attention of the transactive effect of cognitive and affective aspects of concept formation is that of Bower and Hollister (1967). Believing that children develop strong egos in the process of becoming effective learners and vice versa, Bower and Hollister concern themselves with concrete ways in which teachers may strengthen ego processes in children through the curriculum. Hollister gives this process the happy name of "stren" which he regards as an anonym of trauma.

Bower and Hollister identify competence in the use of symbols as one ego skill through which the child can organize, bind and utilize knowledge as a tool to understand the world. Symbolization must be precise enough to yield a

firm construction, yet broad and loose enough to yield creative insights or transformations. Only with ego strength can concepts become organized to the full.
In one trenchant passage Bower (1968) observes:

> Ego processes not only organize and reorganize knowledge and them-
> selves, but can tie or hold on to much knowledge. Symbols are the tools by
> which this magic is accomplished. Without the tools of language and numbers,
> little if any knowledge can be packaged and stored. To tie knowledge effec-
> tively into symbols, the symbols need meaningful conceptual glue.

Then in a brilliant section he identifies five ego processes and shows how teachers
can use the curriculum to build these strens. The five processes are as follows:

a. differentiation (the separation of objects, symbols and feelings)

b. fidelity-distortion (tying symbols to objects, words and actions)

c. pacing versus overloading (regulating inputs and unloading actions)

d. expansion-constriction (seeking new metaphors, meanings and uses)

e. integration-fragmentation (assimilating, interconnecting).

Each of these ego processes enables the child to deal more efficiently with
experience. Fidelity, the representation of the experience in its reality, gives a
truer picture inside the child's mind about what is going on outside. Creativity
rests on the high fidelity of replication of experience. When experience is stereotyped and restricted, little creativity can emerge for it is the high fidelity repro-
duction of experience, rich with multivaried splendor, which gives the best chance
for new combinations or assortments of all the complex parts. Thus the objective
of escalation of developmental process is creative functioning.

The child is a creative generalist. He is not specialized for his wonderment
is everywhere. Escalation requires that he give his attention selectively to an ever-
decreasing and more specialized segment of the totality of his experience so that,
while his creativity may augment, he has as an adult become "type cast" in an
ever-narrowing role. As a college student, he may pick one major; as a graduate
student, he will concentrate in one aspect of that major; as a Ph.D. candidate, he
will single out a small segment of that area for his thesis; and his later professional
writings will be on still more specialized topics. Only rarely does he recapture
the omnivorous wonder that besets the child at every turn, and then only when
rapture or travel transports him to another vivency.

Jourard (1968, p. 2) echoes this idea well in stating:

> The world of experience is constantly disclosing itself to us as it gives
> evidence of continual change. When we form a concept of this process, we
> freeze it in time, and the signals from the changing entity which we are observ-
> ing cease to be perceived by us. To us the object ceases to disclose itself be-
> cause we close our receiving apparatus. Growth is the disintegration of one
> way of experiencing following by a new way of experiencing which includes
> a new disclosure.[1]

---

[1]From page 2, Jourard, S. M. "Growing Awareness and the Awareness of Growth" in Otto,
H. and Mann, J. *Ways of Growth*, Copyright, 1968, Otto and Mann. Used by permission.

If this childish sense of wonder and generalism is the creative genius of our species, one wonders if a super-species some say may produce super-children who as adults will retain this complete curiosity during all of life, as well as a generalized attention which will make them masters of many modes. This indeed was the ideal of the *uomo universale* of the Renaissance, the universal genius of whom Leonardo da Vinci and Goethe are prominent examples. Such men maintain in adulthood (which is like a super-childhood) the same generalized attention to all aspects of the world which continue to utterly fascinate them. These superior individuals may illustrate in their enriched lives the course of evolution for tomorrow and the ages afterward.

Barron (1968, p. 168) sums up this idea very well when he speaks of the usual process of maturation as a personal adjustment that is "normal" but "is achieved at the cost of repression of the spontaneity and wonder of childhood." He feels that the person who is open to experience retains the childhood experience in consciousness and hence integrates its benefits into the total personality.

We may get some insight about the escalation of attention (and the consequent diminution of range) by looking at figure 4 which is designed to represent an individual moving from childhood (left) to seniority (right). The entire power or ability available to the individual is split between two dimensions, a horizontal range or versatility and a vertical mastery or intensity. The cross section representing individual power at any given time is roughly a constant that is, as his range or versatility decreases, his mastery or intensity increases reciprocally. Hence he moves from generalist to specialist with the same total power. Hereditary and environmental influences determine the two personal variables, range and angle of convergence. The result of this life progression is a solid with the top surface curved upward to represent escalation. The child who was a generalist with a wide range of curiosity but low mastery becomes as an adult a specialist with a narrow range of interest but high mastery. If environmental or emotional defects open up the angle of convergence too much, the individual will not have a chance to reach creative heights as an adult before his base becomes so narrow as to preclude further progress. Conversely, if individual interests are narrowed early, he will have a broad enough base to enter higher stages. Hence it is only the superior individual in good mental health who can gain higher states and phases where creative performance can occur.

In this chapter, escalation is described as an aspect of developmental process which involves increasing complexity and embraces five attributes: succession, discontinuity, emergence, differentiation and integration. Succession implies a fixed order within a hierarchy. Discontinuity involves an ordered and discrete sequence of equilibriums. Emergence involves budding and the making of the implicit, explicit. Differentiation refers to the escalatory attribute which clarifies, fixates, and metamorphosizes the emphasis in successive developments. Integration contains a summation of the other attributes into a higher synthesis with greater complexity and new degrees of freedom.

Examples of these processes of escalation were then given with regard to that major task of childhood—concept formation. Duality between cognitive and affective developmental stair cases is featured, and the significance of the

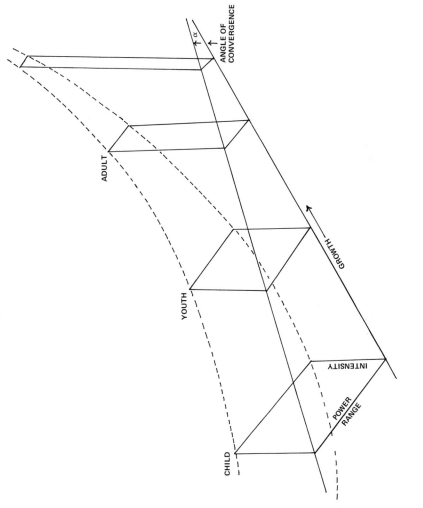

Figure 4. The Escalation of Attention.

transactive relationship between the cognitive and the affective in the child's development is emphasized. The necessity of these processes as the precursors of creativity in the child is discussed, and the objective of escalation is seen as creative performance in the individual. This performance is the subject for chapter 4.

4

CREATIVITY

Everyone who tries to cope effectively and consciously with the developmental tasks of his particular stage of maturity is engaged in a creative task—the work of self-creation. [1]

—Elsa Whalley

CREATIVITY AS THE OUTCOME OF THE PROPER FUNCTIONING OF DEVELOPMENT

We have seen that the objective of escalation is creativity, which is emergent in the personal "unfoldment" of the individual as part of his developmental process. This unfoldment is as natural as the budding and blossoming of a rose, if proper conditions of sunshine, soil and moisture are present. Once a certain developmental stage has been reached, creativity is a direct outcome of self-awareness.

When asked, "What is creativity?", Erich Fromm, distinguished psychoanalyst, replied: "It is the ability to see, to be aware, and to respond" (Mooney and Razik, 1967, p. 44). He continued (*ibid*, p. 53): "... One's own powers to

[1]From page 99, *Humanitas*, 6:1:95–116, Copyright 1970. Used by permission.

be aware and to respond; that is one's own creativity. To be creative means to consider the whole process of life as a process of birth, and not to take any stage of life as a final stage. Most people die before they have been fully born. Creativeness means to be born before one dies."

Creativity itself is an emergent and characteristic outcome of the theory of developmental stages. When the requisite degree of mental health is present, creativity is an inevitable outcome of developmental process. Maslow (Anderson, 1968, p. 84) speaks of creativity as a "universal heritage of every human" and one which "covaries with psychological health." The individual who gains mental health as he goes through the developmental process exhibits increasing creativeness. An individual who experiences strain and anxiety evidences diminished creativity.

The amount of creativity, other things being equal, is a barometer of one's mental health. Maslow (Anderson, 1958, p. 88) elaborates this idea further when he says: "The creativity of my subjects seemed to be an epiphenomenon of their greater wholeness and integration, which is what self-actualized implies." It is as natural to express creativity under conditions of high mental health as it is for a heated black object to radiate electromagnetic waves. At first there is no emanation, then with increasing temperature there is first heat, then light, and finally ultraviolet rays. Here the increase of temperature corresponds to expanded mental health, and the appearance of electromagnetic waves corresponds to creative production.

In a section of *Creativity and Development* Anderson (1959, pp. 121 ff.) amplifies the meaning of differentiation and integration in the development process as having five aspects: (1) confrontation of differences, (2) integration, (3) a yielding up or giving up of the old for a new reorganization, (4) a process of differentiation and (5) a positive directionality. Growth creates differences within the individual and emphasizes his uniqueness from others; these differences are combined into new patterns giving rise to originality; originality is intrinsic in creativity, so creativity is an outcome of development.

A critic may ask: "How can creativity be both an outcome of developmental process and the name of a particular cognitive stage (the sixth)?" Industry is the name given by Erikson to the fourth affective stage, yet no one would feel that this naming precludes an industrious attitude being shown at any other period in life. The reason for the name is that this period emphasized industry, just as the sixth stage emphasizes the cognitive style of creative production. The growing boy is ready to make things in the fourth stage, and ready to use his logical powers in a creative fashion in the sixth stage, It is indeed not surprising that in youthful adulthood when all the individual's powers are at the flood, he should have the best opportunity to be creative.

OEDIPAL ORIGINS: MAGIC NIGHTMARE OR CREATIVE FANTASY

While the individual of enough mental health should be creative at all ages and stages, in reality that creativity is expressed in stage spurts. The genesis of creativity occurs in the third stage (initiative-intuitive) period, when the child is drawn oedipally to the parent of the opposite sex. He may be plunged into a creative fantasy conceptualization of his world through which, with parental help and love, he gains some control over the new forces in his environment or, without parental help, he may experience a magic nightmare when the environment controls him, and he is powerless.

The creative fantasy is apparent in the third stage when an able and healthy child receives the full affectional approach of the opposite sexed parent. Hence, creative individuals tend to have oedipal and electral complexes. Boys who are affectionally close to their mothers and girls who are unusually close to their fathers during the years from four to seven tend to become more creative than others of similar ability. The child in this period responds to the warm affection of the opposite sexed parent by freely enlarging the bridge between his fantasy life and his real world. The affectionate adult who values the child's ideas stimulates and encourages the child to produce ideas and show off intellectually. The emotional support encourages the child to draw freely from past experiences, and to retrieve half-forgotten ideas from the preconscious. Thus he becomes able to dip further into this area and produce more creative ideas than another child whose efforts might be inhibited by his parent's disapproval or negative judgments.

The child's successes in winning the affection from the opposite sexed parent gives some semblance of reality to the oedipal fantasies of this period. The bridge between fantasy and reality becomes strengthened while at the same time the child feels "in control," and he grows in the power to discriminate between what is and what is longed for. This control is perhaps what Kris meant by "regression in the service of the ego." This kind of creativity is exhibitionistic, with intrusive, phallic qualities characteristic of the stage. Because more boys are close to their mothers during this period (closer than girls are to their fathers) may be one explanation why there later are more creative men than women in the world of adults.

At this time the child discovers his individuality in a world of powerful and forbidding adults. He recognizes his wants and impulses and senses the strength of his will which can be satisfied either through action or fantasy. Each may lead to pleasure or pain, to joy or guilt, and to growing power and success or to helpless immobilization. For the child this period can be a creative fantasy or a magic nightmare, on the one hand a full expression of the Sullivanian "good me" and on the other a frightening experience of the "not-me," the resolution depending upon the degree of control he can exert as compared with the controls exerted upon him by the significant adults in his life.

Some of the best loved and most enduring fairy tales throughout the world center around this theme of a child imprisoned in a magic kingdom, surrounded by powerful good and evil personifications, who later prove to be impotent. In *Alice in Wonderland, Through the Looking Glass* and *The Wizard of Oz* a powerful like-sexed figure (the Queen of Hearts, the Red Queen, and the Wicked Witch of the West) attempts to immobilize the child protagonist. After a series of scary adventures aided by weak, male, nonhuman models (the White Rabbit, the White Knight, and Dorothy's three companions), the child triumphs over and reveals the actual impotence of the magical figure. Alice says: "You're nothing but a pack of cards" and herself becomes a queen; Dorothy discovers that even the kindly Wizard of Oz is a fake and gets back to Kansas on her own. This discovery that adults do not actually have the magic powers ascribed to them by the child signals the transformation from the magic nightmare of the third stage to the workaday world of the industry stage.

STABILIZING THE CREATIVE FUNCTION

During the third developmental stage (the initiative period), significant processes occur within the developing child as he is confronted with the following tasks:

a. The child learns whether to defend or cope (Bruner).

b. The child learns the symbolic representation of experience (Bruner).

c. The child moves along the (Rank) continuum from adapted to creative.

d. The child "establishes his preconscious" (Kubie) and learns to operate the creativity cycle.

Let us discuss these in turn.

The Child Learns Whether to Defend or Cope

If you were a knight in a country where there were fire-breathing dragons, you would have two choices. One would be to remain within your castle walls, and defend against the dragons by making the moat deeper and the battlements higher. You could imagine worse and worse dragons until one finally came to get you. On the other hand, you might decide to face the danger and go down fighting. Then you would practice jousting; get the best horse, sword and coat of mail (and asbestos) you could find; and one fine morning ride across the moat prepared to do battle. And if you survived, you would probably find that the dragons were not so bad as they were rumored to be. This is coping.

The writer once talked with a gifted boy about seven who said he had 35 ways of going home from school so that he would not be beaten up by other little boys. When asked how many times he had been beaten up he said "Never," but that was because he had 35 different ways of going home from school. Here was a child so busy defending against imaginary dangers he had little time to cope with the real world.

The Child Learns the Symbolic Representation of Experience

Bruner (1966) tells us that about stage three, children go through the enactive, iconic stages and eventually arrive at symbolic representation of experience. Reaching symbolic representation allows a child to make his experience intellectually negotiable; that is, he can describe and communicate it. With this comes the satisfaction of what Sullivan calls "consensual validation": one can have the relief of finding out that one's experience is not unique and uncanny (part of Sullivan's "not me") but common to others, and hence may be incorporated without fear into the "me." This reassurance enables the child to continue learning because he has enough ego-strength to cope with and reach out for new experience, rather than to withdraw with fear and defend against imaginary dangers.

The symbolic representation of experience is a big feat for any child since it frees him from much of the "nightmare" trauma which precedes consensual validation. It is even a more significant achievement for the gifted child since it involves him in creative fantasy. More exactly, the early mastery of this task while he is still in the third stage (initiative-intuitive period) exposes him to the creative possibilities of his preconscious which are still accessible while he has gained the ability to communicate them verbally.

Our argument is better represented graphically than otherwise. In figure 5, the lower horizontal line represents chronological age and the left, vertical mental age. The first three stages are marked off vertically, and the upper horizontal represents the mental level of symbolic representation (roughly reading readiness) reached for the average child at approximately six and a half years of age. The lower diagonal line represents the growth of the average child which intersects at 6.5 M.A. and C.A. The upper diagonal represents the growth of the superior child, progressing at a sharper slope and reaching the level of symbolic representation for a considerable space while still in the initiative period. Thus this child is able to produce and communicate verbal concepts at a time when he is still highly influenced by fantasy, which gives its special enhancement to his developing verbal creativity. Since IQ is a rough measure of the slope of the diagonal, the minimum slope to get much of this benefit is about 1.2, which may be the reason why verbal creativity seems to demand a threshold of about 120 IQ (1.2 x 100).

The Child Moves Somewhere Along the Continuum from Adapted to Creative

We learned in chapter 1 something about the views of the psychoanalyst Otto Rank regarding adapted, conflicted and creative growth. The child enters stage three (the initiative period) with some ego reserves from stage two (the autonomy period). He has learned that he is not part of his mother and that he can on occasion successfully oppose her. The will, primitively developed in the autonomy period, flowers fully in the next stage when the child becomes master of his body and finds it a source of never-ending energy. This period brings a thrusting initiative which carries the child into multiple dimensions of discovery. In the previous stage, his occasional failures to meet societal demands (such as toileting) was a vice, for it was something over which he had little, if any, control. Doubt and shame were bad enough. But now the child discovers that in this wonderful Garden of Eden there is the serpent of sin, engendered by his will when he makes the wrong choice. This discovery invests choice making (as

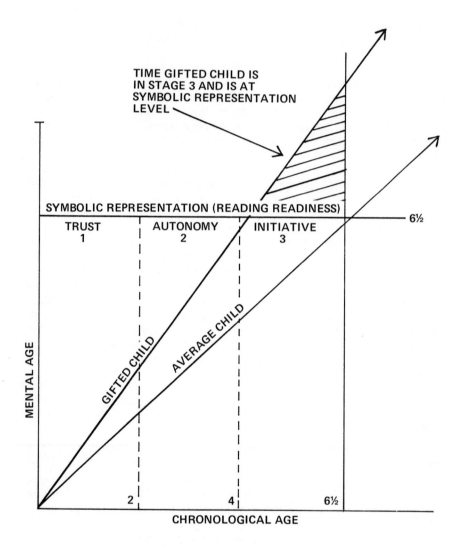

*Figure 5. Diagram Showing Why Gifted Child Is More Likely
to be Verbally Creative*

opposed to strict obedience to parental demands), with special dangers—the danger of fear and guilt, the danger of anxiety, and most of all the danger of being immobilized and not being cherished—the Sullivanian "bad me."

The joy and sheer delight which the child finds in all kinds of new and creative discoveries is now balanced by the remorse, guilt and anxiety which is brought home to him by punishment for some of these forbidden efforts. ("You must not touch or take this; you must not say that; you must not do the other thing.") Thus the development of initiative brings joy and satisfaction on one side and guilt and immobilization on the other.

The child who is too thoroughly frightened by his mistakes and by parental prohibitions at this stage will give up; he may decide it is best to be completely docile and not risk any painful consequences. In time he will learn to conform automatically, not even for expedience, and this guilt induced immobilization or conformity will later be extended from judgmental parents to a prescriptive school, to a religious creed and an authoritarian society. In later life this man, conscientious but pathetic, will write poignantly in his memoirs, as die the late George Apley, "You can't escape Boston."

Many children are stronger than this and persist in reaching out to find values and experiences other than those sanctioned by parents. Those who fight alone or with minimum adult support feel very "conflicted," to use Rank's phrase. Eternally obsessed with guilt feelings, they develop neurotic tendencies always to fight or flee. And while the neurosis is positive in that it shows the fight is still going on, it is fatal or nearly so for the creative impulse. For the energy which should go into productivity goes instead into waging the war within or fighting "The Inner Conflict," and this is indeed what Kubie (1958) means by *The Neurotic Distortion of the Creative Process.*

Finally there is the lucky creative child who somehow wins through neurotic involvement to find most of his creative potential intact. This may be due to the affectional support of the opposite sexed parent, whose warmth puts a higher valence on creative activities, and enables the child to uncover and make available his preconscious areas within the ego's reach. The close relationship also blunts the threat of parental prohibition and convinces the child that fewer things are denied and that more things are possible and permitted.

The fantasy of this period which seems to remain in the preconscious of the average child is brought more into reality by the bright child. Whereas, through fear and repression of the experience as a magic nightmare, many children seem to have almost aborted this stage of development, the creative child seems able to bring more of this experience from the "not me" to the "good me" area. He almost seems to have overstayed his leave in this kingdom, and its door to fantasy is always left slightly ajar. The loving parent has provided a wide and safe platform for consensual validation. When the child reports having seen a fire-breathing dragon, for instance, the mother does not scold him for telling a lie, but asks playfully "What color was it?" As with the trauma of birth, very few children come through these stages completely unscathed. And so the creative youngster is apt to retain a superabundance of joy, activity and discovery, only to pay for this outburst of energy by a cyclic slack time characterized by guilt, resentment or immobilization. Thus parental reactions during the third stage of initiative has helped mold the child into one of the types described by Rank as adapted, conflicted or creative.

The Child Establishes the Preconscious and Learns to Operate the Creativity Cycle

Growth toward new conceptualization or creative reorganization requires the release of the present conceptualization resulting in a fluid state out of which arises a new and higher organization. An old concept too restricted to accommodate new experiences must be adjusted much as one would slip out of a tight pair of shoes, wander around in the grass for awhile in one's bare feet and then get into a new and larger pair. Psychologically, relaxation of a rigid cognitive structure is accomplished through free play which somehow disengages the too tightly bound concept and hands the whole business to the preconscious. The preconscious in some manner reorganizes the construction and enlarges it and, under suitable conditions, leaks the salient aspects of the reorganization back to the conscious mind. The psychotherapy slogan "unfreeze, change, and refreeze" applies here. Free play unfreezes the concept and makes it fluid. The preconscious changes it, and the new concept is again refrozen into the cognitive structure. Let us investigate this critical process in some detail.

Piaget (1951, pp. 147–50) states: "The underlying structure of play is constituted by a certain reorientation of the ego to reality." Ruitenbeek (1965, p. 16) tells us that "In *Creative Writers and Daydreaming*, Freud explored the connection between the imaginative play of childhood and the fantasizing of later life. . . ." Sadler (1969) equates play with creative perception and advocates play as a pathway to personal freedom. Kubie (1958, p. 56) remarks on the application of free association to creativity: "In psychological affairs, free associations are our Gallup Poll" (that is, they sample what is going on in the mind). He continues:

> Creativity itself depends upon the process of free association which makes possible preconscious analogic processes yet at the same time exposes them to deformation under the influence of concurrent unconscious processes.[1]

Sadler (1969) in investigating playful perception, notes the relationship of focal attention to the development of a healthy creative personality. He says:

> It is also a perceptual mode that pertains to play. The creative edge of perception whereby we remain open and sensitive to new meanings and increasing awareness of life possibilities originates in and is sustained through play. . . .
> Play reveals itself as a basic existential form to keep one's world open, not defensively, but creatively.[2]

---

[1] From page 56, Kubie, Lawrence S., *The Neurotic Distortion of the Creative Process*, Copyright, 1958, University of Kansas Press. Used by permission.

[2] From Sadler, W. A., "Creative Existence: Play as a Pathway to Personal Freedom," Copyright, *Humanitas*, 5:57–80, 1969. Used by permission.

Getzels and Jackson (1962, p. 99) refer to this sense of playfulness in their subjects as follows:

> It is almost as if the creative adolescents experience a special delight in playful intellectual activity for its own sake. They involve themselves in the game-like task . . . seemingly because of the intrinsic pleasure that accompanies their use of fantasy.[1]

The importance of play as an avenue to the preconscious is highlighted by Koestler (1964), who devotes an entire chapter to "Playing and Pretending" in *The Act of Creation*. The playful and preconscious aspects of creative behavior are further explored in the symposium issue of *Daedalus* by Kubie (1965, p. 565 ff). In another place Kubie (1958, p. 39) tells us that the free play of preconscious process simultaneously accomplishes two goals:

> 1. It supplies an endless stream of old data rearranged into new combinations of wholes and fragments on grounds of analogic elements;
> 2. It exercises a continuous selective influence not only on free associations, but also on the minutiae of living, thinking, walking, talking, dreaming, and indeed every moment of life.[2]

Lieberman (1967, p. 395) even notes that there are two kinds of play:

> The young child's playfulness, and the playfulness outside the play situation shown by the adolescent. . . .
> Both the kindergartner and the adolescent represent important age points for the identification and encouragement of divergent thinking. In the preschool years, one might say that spontaneity flows uncensored by the logical operations, which mature after eleven.

Lieberman feels that the necessity to toy with ideas and relationships may be one factor separating the two kinds of play. It is remarkable how Lieberman's opinions confirm what has earlier been asserted here about the emphasis on creativity in stages three and six, with two kinds of creative production consequent. Her thesis connects this difference with the difference in play, whereas ours is a somewhat wider view, but it is obvious that play and free association form one concomitant of the "I-thou" relationship out of which the creative process emerges. Lieberman in her own research (1965) notes confirmatory evidence from Wallach and Kogan (1965) and Jackson and Messick (1964) and connects playfulness with a sense of humor, a personality correlate often noted in creative persons.

Harold Greenwald (Otto and Mann, 1969, p. 16) explains it well:

> Play on the other hand is by its very nature creative. One of the few really outstanding teachers I once had defined art as "concentrated play."[3]

---

[1]From page 99, Getzels, J. W., and Jackson, P. W. *Creativity and Intelligence*, Copyright 1962, John Wiley & Sons, New York. Used by permission.

[2]From page 39, Kubie, L. L., *The Neurotic Distortion of the Creative Process*, Copyright 1958, University of Kansas Press. Used by permission.

[3]From page 16, Greenwald, H., "Play and Self-Development," Otto, H. A., and Mann, J., *Ways of Growth*, Copyright 1968, Otto and Mann. Used by permission.

In the same article Greenwald quotes Otto as distinguishing seven kinds of play: (1) the spontaneous play of a child, (2) adult play with children, (3) play with animals, (4) play with nature (such as rolling in the grass), (5) primitive play (making mud pies), (6) thrill play (speeding, skiing or flying) and (7) mastery play (sports). To which we would add (8) sexual play, (9) fantasy play (reveries, day-dreams, etc.), (10) mimetic play (in which the same process is repeated or re-hearsed), (11) hobbies (stamp collecting) and (12) unconscious play (rubbing coins together in one's pocket as an unconscious outlet for tension).

The common elements here are: (a) the exhibition of nonutilitarian energy, (b) being in a relaxed or regressed mode, (c) deemphasizing the cognitive and controlling aspects and (d) inviting preconscious and unconscious flux. It is not surprising that among the outcomes of play are a restoration of joy and satisfaction, a realigned conceptual stance which has resulted from the freeing and flow of previously anchored concepts and a residual seepage of reorganized and hence creative ideas from the preconscious into the conscious mind.

This process of regression to the preconscious through free play and day-dreaming fantasy apparently gets its start during the third (initiative stage) when the child with an oedipal or electral attachment to the parent of the opposite sex develops this ability to dip into the preconscious to bring back creative ideas. The key factors in this process are first the courage to explore this "nightmare" area with its uncanny "not-me" aspects, and the second the attentional shift through fantasy and free play to garner peripheral concepts from the preconscious. Kubie (1958) in his masterpiece, *The Neurotic Distortion of the Creative Process,* first stressed the importance of this preconscious function in creative production. He states that preconscious processes are attacked by both superego and ego pro-hibitions, and by unconscious drives. Somehow the preconscious has to grow healthy enough to ward off these attacks and still fulfill its capacity to select and rearrange the data of experience into creative and innovative forms. Kubie believes that the preconscious part of the psyche is the major source of man's creative abilities.

By "establishing the preconscious" we mean the practice of making pre-conscious experience easily available to the reach of the ego, and of bolstering the preconscious (through use) against the attacks of the other aspects of the psyche. The child through exercising his fantasy to please his mother learns implicitly the rules of relaxation, free association and play, which are requisite for him to gain access into this shadowed area.

With much repression the psyche involves a weak preconscious, barricaded from assaults from either side, and a large area of unconscious motivation, unavail-able to conscious use. Little of past experience is available in adaptive behavior. With freedom from threat and supportive parental relations, the preconscious is enlarged at the expense of the unconscious; consequently much more of past experience becomes available for ego use.

Figure 6 illustrates the similarity with which various writers have described the tripartite compartments of the psyche. Freud used three terms: unconscious, preconscious and conscious, and others used similar tri-polar divisions. Thus Sullivan (1965, p. 161) describes similar functions as "bad-me," "not-me" and

TRIPARTITE DIVISION OF THE PSYCHE	BASIC AMORAL "ANIMAL" DRIVES	INNER PARANORMAL "UNCANNY" ASPECTS	SELF-CONSCIOUS EGO-PROCESSES
FREUD	Unconscious "ID"	Preconscious	Conscious "EGO"
SULLIVAN	"Bad-Me"	"Not-Me"	"Good-Me"
EXISTENTIALISM	Umwelt	Eigenwelt	Mitwelt
RELIGIOUS	Animal	Divine	Human

Figure 6. Tripartite Division of the Psyche.

"good-me." "Bad-me" is more conscious than Freud's construct, but is organized as a process variable around increasing anxiety, whereas "not-me" designates frightening, uncanny experience such as those encountered in dreams, nightmares and dissociated behavior. "Good-me" is, of course, a part of conscious positive self concept.

Turning to the existentialists (Ford and Urban, 1963, pp. 455–56), one finds a similar configuration. *Umwelt* is the world of animal drives; *Eigenwelt* is the inner world of man's mind, evolving and becoming; and *Mitwelt* is the world of conscious human personal relationships. A country parson would have no difficulty in characterizing these three modes; his terms would be "animal," "divine" and "human."

In these three divisions of mind we find (1) unconscious and basically amoral biological impulses and drives, (2) self-conscious ego processes and (3) inner, paranormal, "uncanny" aspects. One is immediately reminded of Bucke's divisions of consciousness (1923, p. 1) into (1) simple consciousness (characteristic of animals), (2) self-consciousness (characteristic of humans) and (3) cosmic consciousness (rudimentary in a few humans, but evolving to become a future characteristic of a finer species).

Such a view immediately suggests our previous argument, namely that the preconscious is the source of man's creativity, particularly when it is strengthened, protected and enlarged through regular use and through increasing mental health. The "establishment" of the preconscious is evidence that the individual is not at war with himself, not alienated from experience, not a split personality. He can be creative because almost all his past experiences, in chewed-up and digested form, ready to be reattached to new concepts, are available to his preconscious collator. It has at its disposal a vast assortment of biological impulses, tabooed acts, rejected compromises, affective pains and pleasures, remembered facts, personal feelings, horrifying nightmares and a host of other material, none of which has been suppressed, but all of which can be reused (much like old newspapers) to print a new edition. What is in the new edition depends on how much freedom the editor (preconscious) has from the incursions of the prohibitions of the conscious and super-ego and the pressures of experiences and feelings suppressed by the unconscious. The health, growth and stability of the preconscious thus becomes of prime importance in investigating the genesis of creativity.

With this in mind, the inspection of figure 7 (adapted from Kubie, 1968) is invited, in which the conscious, preconscious and unconscious are displayed in diagram form from right to left, and the diagrams down the page feature a growth in mental health as well as a growth laterally of the preconscious at the expense of both the conscious and the subconscious.

Each diagram illustrates the relationship between conscious, preconscious and unconscious portions of the psyche in differing individuals from very sick (top) to very well (bottom). In the first instance (the psychotic), the preconscious has vanished under pressure from the external pressures of the conscious and the taboos of the unconscious; the other two portions have broken apart, resulting in a split personality. In the second diagram (the neurotic) the preconscious, while diminished under buffeting from the conscious and the unconscious,

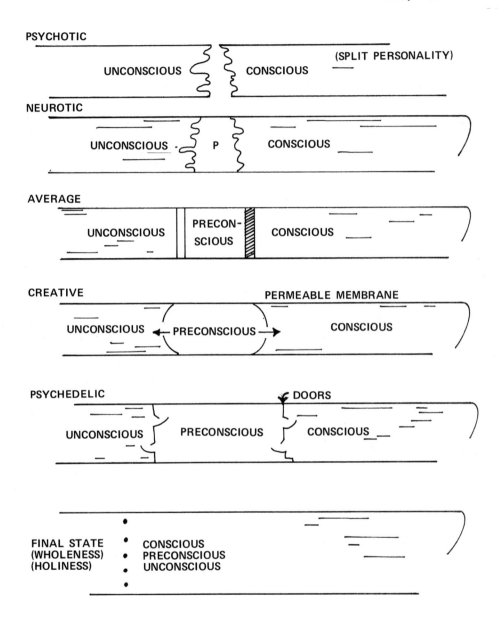

Figure 7. Development of the Preconscious

still managed to exist and hold the personality together. In the third diagram (the average), a thick impenetrable wall has been established, protecting the preconscious but compartmentalizing the psyche and preventing intercommunication. In the fourth diagram (the creative), the preconscious is healthy and expanded enough so that the walls have been replaced by a permeable membrane through which, under osmotic pressure, ideas filter through to the conscious and subconscious. In the fifth diagram (the psychedelic), the preconscious has grown in extent, and the membrane has been replaced by doors which swing open, giving the ego direct contact with the preconscious and hence a feeling of strangeness and expansion. In the last diagram (illumination), the three aspects are merged into a continuous state of wholeness.

The essence of process toward both greater mental health and greater creativity lies in the strengthening and developing of the preconscious so that it enlarges to assume a more important share in the tripartite membership of the individual psyche. This aggrandizement signals improved mental health and progress toward self-actualization, of which creative performance is an early indication. McLuhan and the existentialists emphasize a better balance between rational and pararational aspects of the psyche, and perhaps in this instance they are merely restating the thesis which has just been illustrated here.

A good deal of space has been devoted to a full explanation of the function of play and retrieval through free association and fantasy to "establish the preconscious": as a healthy, working, viable member of the psyche, able to protect its boundaries, and more easily available to the use of the ego. But now it must be emphasized that this is the beginning, not the end, of a developing creative life style which will escalate in future stages to gain new repertoires and techniques. The child will learn, for example, implicitly to follow the Wallas stages of preparation, incubation, illumination and verification. His ego will grow bolder and more courageous in encounters with the preconscious. Finally, he will also discover that the process of creative production is a cycle in which the positive amplitude is creativity, and the nonproductive part of the cycle need not result in negative or destructive reactions to self or others, but should be used for rest and relaxation. But the beginnings in "establishing the preconscious" are crucial. Kubie sums it up when he states (1959, p. 143): "Creativity is a product of preconscious activity. This is the challenge which confronts the education of the future."[1]

Creativity would be a more common experience if only the preconscious were not such a formidable phantasmagoria to deal with. A creative masterpiece may represent a supreme effort to resolve or at least to deal with a frightening "not me" conflict that even a recurrent nightmare cannot exorcise. Mack (1970, p. 94) believes that terrifying dreams and nightmares are particularly likely to result in creative production, especially if the ego is able to master the situation and not be intimidated by it. As Mack states (1970, p. 99): "Creativity and madness are two alternatives to nightmares, or more accurately to the critical

---

[1]From page 143, Kubie, Lawrence S., *The Neurotic Distortion of the Creative Process*, Copyright 1968, University of Kansas Press. Used by permission.

conflicts which give rise to them." The difference, he goes on to point out, lies in the hold on reality which the artist has because art, as Kris (1952) has pointed out, is related to the degree of intactness of the ego.

In the ballet *Coppelia*, when Swanhilde and her companions venture into the dark atelier of Dr. Coppelius, she encounters a frightening array of automatons in menacing positions. Only gradually as her fear ebbs, does she grasp the creative possibilities of the situation. In a similar manner, the preconscious is a dark repository of the leftover stage props of living; and when we venture into this darkened and chaotic property room of our minds, we, like Swanhilde, may be in for a good scare, or, if we have courage and cleverness, we may be able to put the props together into a new play, fantasy or creation. Mack (1970, p. 99) believes that "creative ability can be a powerful integrating force" to restore stability and balance after a frightening exposure of the ego to the "not me" of the preconscious.

Greenacre (1962) in discussing creativity in adults, points out that its manifestation may relieve but not solve conflicts. And Mack (1970, p. 180) feels that "we should perhaps measure psychological health by a capacity . . . to achieve fruitful accommodations." Robert Louis Stevenson, an extremely creative author, who in his private life often seemed regressed in the oedipal period, tells us how he converted nightmares into some of his many fanciful stories (1909). Beset by nightmares, he discovered that he could impose his will on these preconscious experiences and, by modifying and shaping them to the demands of his ego, he could convert them into useful literary products. The key question in the encounter with the dark, dissociated forms of the "not me" is whether the ego will be daunted and immobilized and forced to let its energies out in dreams, nightmares and psychotic episodes, or whether by a supreme act of will it can create, out of the seeming chaos, a new and higher order.

STAGE RELATIONSHIPS OF CREATIVITY

The previous section has dwelt on the vital role of stage three (initiative) in the development of creative performance. But it should also be noted that figure 1 in chapter 2 suggests that the sixth stage (intimacy) has special potential for creative adults. Society and young adults in the sixth stage are often so concerned and involved over the sexual aspects of the period that the possibilities it affords for creative arousal are missed altogether. The gifts of countless artists, poets and musicians have flowered in this stage, generally in direct response to the inspiration of a beloved companion. Dante, Byron, and Wagner are three well-known examples, but Galois and Arriaga, geniuses who died before reaching their majority, are even more appropriate illustrations. A peculiar property of this stage in outstandingly creative persons lies in a tempering of oncoming aging, in keeping the artist youthful, often in appearance, and always in spirit. We shall try to analyze this phenomenon more thoroughly in later chapters.

It is interesting that Erikson (Evans, 1966, p. 57) appears to locate this second burst of creativity in the generativity (seventh) stage instead of the sixth.

Talking about the reasons for the term he says:

> If I would call this strength creativity, I would put too much emphasis on the particular creativity which we ascribe to particular people. I use generativity, because I mean everything that is generated: children, products, ideas and works of art.[1]

While Creativity Is Emphasized at Stages Three and Six, It Is Not Absent at Other Stages

We tend to create for those we love. The motivational pressures resulting from oedipal love at stage three and heterosexual love at stage six power the creativity surges at these stages. Being different in flavor, each stage gives rise to different kinds of creativity. But once a creative style of life has been established through contact with the preconscious, processes and techniques tend to persist as strategies available to the ego. They may even expand and proliferate at any stage under suitable conditions of mental health and environmental stimulation.

Creative performance is the synthesis of several independent systems:

(a)   differential abilities and their stimulation as in the Guilford structure of intellect model

(b)   mental and physical health

(c)   antiauthoritarian and nurturing tendencies in parents and others in the environment

(d)   the life styles established in the third and sixth stages of development.

The first three can occur at any time in human life. Tendencies toward creative performance, especially those influenced by education, can and do occur at all stages of development.

The shift and reorganization of concepts required as the child goes from one cognitive level to another may demand energy or impose strain which temporarily diminishes creative performance. This may explain why Torrance (1962, 1964) has found that there are drops at fourth and seventh grade in creativity test scores, since these grades mark the onset of new developmental stages. Such higher cognitive stages, however, as "categorizing" in the concrete operations stage and "if then" contingency in the formal operations stage add new degrees of freedom to ego functioning, and this escalation gives the possibility of higher and more complex productions.

Creativity Occurs in Individuals of Less Than Perfect Mental Health Even Though Mental Health Enhances Creative Performance

The creative person is not necessarily perfect and without flaw. Actually, creativity occurs rather early in the development of the mentally healthy individual and promises the continuation of such mental health, much as ego strength

---

[1]From page 57, Evans, R. I., *Dialog With Erik Erikson,* Copyright 1967, Harper & Row Publishers. Used by permission.

measures predict the successful termination of therapy. Creative performance tends to influence development in the direction of mental health, as fruit on a tree or dividends on a stock promise the future vitality of an organism. Hence almost all children are creative, but few adults are. Adverse conditions or circumstances may deny the early promise, or the playful creativity of the child may not have been bolstered with the cognitive task structure necessary to produce the more formal and finished productions of adult creativity. Childish creativity requires only playfulness; adult creativity requires discipline.

Developmental process with moderate environmental stimulation and some openness in the life style carry the child naturally toward creative expression through adolescence. The problem is to remain creative after the biological push to development is over at sexual maturity. This is when "normal" people go to seed. Those adults who continue to be creative preserve their creative drives by a simultaneous search for greater amounts of mental health and for environments which stimulate and enhance creative response. We shall discuss details of this search in the next chapter.

Creativity enhances mental health in the adult, but in adults, as in children, creative insights often come before the power to nurture the idea and follow through with it is gained. Most of us have creative ideas on occasion, as most women occasionally become pregnant. But whereas many women carry the fetus full term and have the baby, most of us continually abort the creative ideas and never bring them to fruition.

Creativity is not a rare experience accessible only to genius. It is a natural and indeed an inevitable outcome of an intelligent mind when functioning in conditions of desirable mental health. Every inward (preconscious) state has an inherent tendency to form, but it lies supine until revitalized and expressed by the attention of the conscious mind. This pressing outward imprints on the latent plastic state the cognitive properties of the conscious mind, the creative vision of the preconscious and the limitations of the unconscious. The visible product is, therefore, colored by the author's views which may be idiosyncratic and imperfect. The knack of creativity is not only in "turning on" the potency of the preconscious mind which nurtures the idea, but also in the art of "turning on" nontrivially, so that the new creation may be truly new, worthy and consequential and not tarnished with imitation and imperfection. We find these latter elements particularly in the child's first attempt to be creative, and teachers, parents and guidance personnel need help in raising the child's sights so that the product will not be new merely to the child (and repetitious to the culture), but also original enough to be new and truly innovative for all.

Every creative accomplishment is an actualization of an "impossible dream," a visible outpicturing of an inward state; it is, therefore, sacramental in the truest sense. But its shock of recognition and "effective surprise" depends upon even more than this; namely, that it contains within itself the bud or nucleus of a vision of perfection and of further progress toward it. This final emanation of grace gives the creative act its characteristic and indefinable charm, for it not only contains the happy and explicit solution to a present problem, but an implicit promise of growth toward an even higher resolution.

After a careful case study investigation of the influence of mental health on creativity Fried (1964) concluded that increased mental health as established through therapy improved artistic work habits, freed and sublimated aggressive, destructive tendencies into productive work patterns, reduced omnipotent fantasy which had caused the artists to destroy many of their works which were below the masterpiece level, and improved human relations which tended to preserve creative energy. The creativity increase in these artists undergoing therapy appeared as an early dividend resulting from their increased mental health.

CREATIVITY AS EVOLUTIONARY DEVELOPMENT: THROWBACKS AND THROW-FORWARDS

Creativity is a characteristic not only of individual human behavior, but also of the species in general. What is true of the development of the superior individual is also true of the developing aspects of mankind. The emergence of creative abilities is a triumph not only of individual development but, as Bucke (1929) points out, the harbinger of evolutionary progress for all men. Astronaut Armstrong echoed these ideas when he first stepped onto the moon: "One small step for a man; one giant step for mankind."

In the grand progression of evolutionary life, each man has a small degree of freedom because he can choose within limits to ride in the van or bring up the rear. The atavist in society is a throwback to former days, a reconceptualization of the past. The creative man, by contrast, is an earnest of the future, a throw-forward to a better time and humanity. He constitutes an implicit and intuitive statement of powers yet to be fully apprehended by the species. That his clutch on these powers is sometimes weak and spasmodic should not bother us, for it was Browning who said: "A man's reach should exceed his grasp, else what's a heaven for?"

The sense of destiny, of being caught up in process toward the future, a quality exhibited by many creative or self-actualized people, is part of an existential act of becoming in which one is thrown forward into the living actualization of one's potentialities. One becomes in flux like the electron in orbit, having energy and momentum but no position or fixity.

Hallman (1963) speaks of this sense of worth and destiny as follows:

> The third set of meanings contained in the criterion of openness points to the need of the creative personality to have a sense of personal destiny and worth which will allow him to accept himself as the source of values. It is obvious that anyone who tolerates uncertainties and conflicts for long must enjoy an anchorage within some value system apart from the conventional order, and this would need to be himself. The forward-looking search for possibilities which characterizes the creative process implies an acceptance of self as a source of judgment. The new creations exist at first in the future and in tentative form; they exist as possibilities. If they become original creations, they must take on the values which the individual assigns to them. Since the creative person must speculate, test, modify, and postpone completion of his work, he needs to rely on his own sensitivity for guidance.

The guilt-immobilized, uncreative (reactive) individual is transparent and easily recognized. His dress, manner and attitude betray stress, fixity and stasis. He is role typed, not versatile; tense, not relaxed; uneasy, not confident; superstitious, not flexible; bound, not free; phlegmatic, not buoyant; static, not dynamic; stolid, not energetic; dull, not scintillating; dowdy, not chic; inhibited, not spontaneous; inert, not active; self-conscious, not selfless; discouraged, not happy; and an object of sympathy rather than personally appealing.

Life is more than mere intervals between trips to the toilet; it can be intervals between trips to the stars. Is it more meaningful to regard man as a reactive being or as a creative mind? If man is a reactive being, a mere brute creature imprisoned in a universe for which he has no responsibility, he is much like the steer that grazes the plain and, like the steer, he will end up butchered. But if man has a creative mind, he has a part in the noumenon of that creation and, in the alternation of that open-ended universe, he can intervene constructively in his own future and in the future of his species.

Creativity is the process of transforming the horrors and fears of the Sullivanian "not me" into a productive fantasy in the preconscious mind. There is a magic aura to this transformation in which the critical question is whether the ego is to be controlled and immobilized by this frightening environment (as one is in nightmares), or whether the ego through the help of a powerful parental figure is able to organize this apparent chaos, control these magic elements and transform them into a creative fantasy, replacing horror with harmony.

Shakespeare illustrates both the process and the product of this metamorphosis in Ariel's song:

> *Full fathom five thy father lies*
> *Of his bones are coral made;*
> *Those are pearls that were his eyes;*
> *Nothing of him that doth fade*
> *But doth suffer a sea change*
> *Into something rich and strange;*
> *Sea nymphs hourly ring his knell;*
> *Hark, I hear them; Ding-Dong Bell.*
>
> *—The Tempest,* I; 2

Here Ariel represents the ego, aided by the parental figure of Prospero, the good magician. Out of the substance of a drowned cadaver (surely a most horrible object), there is nothing "but doth suffer a sea change/into something rich and strange." The horror, dread and uncanniness of the "not me" become muted and transformed into value, approbation and beauty, and the end result is creative fantasy in its ultimate form.

5

THE CONDITIONS
FOR CREATIVITY:
ENVIRONMENTAL
STIMULATION

The world is too much with us: late and soon,
Getting and Spending we lay waste our powers;
Little we see in nature that is ours;
We have given our hearts away, a sordid boon. . . .
. . . . Great God, I'd rather be
A pagan, suckled by a creed outworn
So might I, standing on this pleasant lea,
Have glimpses which would make me less forlorn
Have sight of Proteus rising from the sea,
Or hear old Triton blow his wreathed horn.

—William Wordsworth

CREATIVE DEVELOPMENT

The creative development of the individual is even more difficult than the dilemma envisioned by Wordsworth, for he must abstract the best in both the world and nature without becoming stultified by the aspects of either. Biological development, which has secured the individual's creativity up to maturity, is no longer available. For further development, continual environmental stimulation is necessary. Perhaps a better way of putting this idea is to say that the forces which act on an individual to produce creativity (such as development and education) are largely outside the individual's control before his majority, but afterward they depend almost exclusively upon himself. Because the unifying process of developmental function has not been fully understood, this important principle has been slighted. In particular, it has not been realized that the more complex developmental processes reached by a few through their intense reactions to enriched environmental stimulation offer a promise of future development for the many.

Two developmental principles have been indicated heretofore as in operation:

(1)   Functions which emerge spasmodically or periodically at earlier stages may be performed more regularly or continuously at higher stages.

(2)   An accomplishment held tenuously only in conditions of peak experience or great mental health will in later development persevere and be present under conditions of more stress.

(3)   Performance reached first by a few superior individuals in a culture will later be reached by more, and, eventually, by the representative members of the culture.

(4)   What first appears as a phenomenon gradually becomes a norm.

This is certainly the time for some thoughtful reader to ask why it is necessary to talk about superior individuals at all if one is discussing a developmental problem. This question deserves a careful answer.

(1)   By superior individual we mean an individual of superior intelligence which would place him in the top two stanines or the upper 11 percent. (It is indeed possible that the future will go to an operational definition of giftedness which is that a "gifted" child is one that has the potentiality to become creative. If this is true, the definition of giftedness on the IQ scale will need to be dropped to about 120, or top 10 to 11 percent.) The basis of experience indicates that these individuals are more likely to become self-actualized than others. Maslow (1954, pp. 202–03), in his famous study, picked no historical figures who were not in this category; indeed, it would be difficult to describe a self-actualized cretin. Let the reader pick his own candidate for self-actualization and then discover if he is not of this level of intelligence.

(2)   Such individuals appear to have a longer mental growth span than others. They appear to continue growing in mental age even into their seniority (whereas others decline) according to the Terman study (1954) followup, which found mental age still increasing at age 50.

(3)   Superior individuals seem to have a "higher ceiling," permitting them access into higher developmental stages which ordinary people seldom attain. This is like "overdrive" on an expensive car.

(4)   Superior individuals accomplish cognitive tasks more quickly and hence go through stages more thoroughly. They, therefore, develop more fully during their life span than do others.

(5)   The mental capacities of the superior individual help him with cognitive tasks, just as improved mental health helps him with affective tasks; both are needed to meet the dual nature of developmental stages.

(6)   Superior individuals first reach new levels of performance and exhibit them only spasmodically or tenuously. Later in evolutionary progress, such attainment will be reached by more individuals and eventually by representative individuals in a culture. It is to the development of the superior individual, therefore, that we must look for a clue to the future developmental potential of the species.

The development of creativity requires abilities identified in the structure of intellect model and a high degree of mental health. Assuming that these two aspects are present in the individual, let us now turn our attention to the problem of adequate environmental stimulation of the individual during different developmental stages. This stimulation will be considered in relation to four educational influences: parental, public school, the university and environmental stimulation of the adult. Much has been written recently about the importance of very early stimulation in the child's development (Hunt, 1961). Instead of repeating this emphasis, we shall proceed with practical suggestions for parents, teachers and counselors, university personnel, and the adult who wishes to preserve and enhance his creativity.

PARENTAL STIMULATION OF CREATIVITY

Developing a Fostering Attitude

Parents can help gifted children to become creative by developing "a fostering attitude." A father who is interested in baseball develops a fostering attitude about baseball for his eight-year-old son by talking to him about baseball, buying him a bat, glove and ball, by playing catch with him, and by showing interest when the son joins a little league. This combination of expectancy and encouragement builds the background of early success experience and the confidence and eagerness which puts the boy in the mood to want to play baseball and to become increasingly successful at that sport. We need to do the same type of thing with regard to helping bright children become creative. We do not start in by setting up an unfavorable evaluation which derides any early manifestations of creativity. Creative performance is not going to occur in a child unless he feels secure enough to try new things. Some ways of providing a fostering attitude are shown in the following:

(1)   Do not belittle the child's first efforts; be sympathetic to his first abortive attempts to create. Upgrade rather than belittle the child's self-concept of his ability to create while remaining relatively realistic about valuing products of his creative effort.

(2)   Provide a warm and safe psychological base from which to explore and to which to return when the child may become frightened by his own discoveries. The mother who allows her child some risk in a new situation, but stays near

so that he can return quickly when he is upset, is an example. Psychological safety is necessary before we can take the risk creativity implies.

(3)   Become accepting of new ideas yourself. Respect children's curiosity and questioning and their ideas. Seek to answer their questions. If ideas or questions are too wild, try to get the child to rephrase them in somewhat sharper or more realistic terms. Instead of saying: "That's silly or impossible," say, "It would be easier to answer that question if you took this fact into consideration."

(4)   Provide stimulating experiences of cultural, social or motor nature to feed new and challenging facts to the child's attention. This can be accomplished, of course, by taking children on trips, outings and excursions. When children have digested the data and are ready to process them, be receptive of their ideas.

(5)   Help children name and classify things. Give them a sense of order and meaning, but do not tell them the whole answer by suggesting where this and that fact may go to form part of the jigsaw puzzle. In helping children value their ideas, attach meaning, worth and value to as many ideas and life experiences as possible.

(6)   Sensory awareness of children may be heightened by helping them to appreciate and enjoy sensory perceptions and experiences without the guilt of feeling that they are somehow "sissy." Parents can point out to children the beauty of simple things, the joy of observing nature closely (such as a spider's web in the sunlight), the delight in crafts (such as weaving) or the pleasure in the mastery of a discipline (such as horseback riding). Children need guides in strange territory so that the strangeness will change to beauty; thus we should help children to half close their eyes to visualize a landscape in its softness, help them to dwell on the beauty and symmetry of a snowflake through a magnifying glass or look at the perfection in a small flower in the desert.

(7)   Remember the really critical question for children to become creative rather than guilt-immobilized is: "Am I in control of my environment through the support of my beloved, or is my environment in control of me?" Hence mothers should seek to reward and support the creative efforts of their young sons and fathers, of their young daughters. Such support gives the child a feeling that the strange fantasy-type world he seems to move in is denuded of its terrors, witches and goblins and is a place to experience a creative fantasy rather than to suffer a magic nightmare.

(8)   It is easy to think of what adults can do to stamp out creative behavior. Think of some of these behaviors and then try to act oppositely.

(9)   Respect individual differences. Do not merely tolerate them. We are glad people are different. We do not just put up with the fact. We are flexible enough to accept children as worthwhile whatever talents they may have.

(10)   Encourage rather than belittle. Walt Disney once did a short movie about a little bug that wanted to change into another kind of a little bug because his lady love was of the latter species. The bug, aided by a fairy godmother, got halfway through the transformation and then got stuck; whereupon a third little

bug, rather a nasty type, sang a little song which went something like: "You're nothing but a nothing; you're not a thing at all." So often parents and other adults, by their actions as well as words, say to a child: "You're nothing but a nothing; you're not a thing at all," and, in consequence, the child sees himself as someone who cannot and does not perform.

(11)   We need to help children in these discontinuities of self-concept. The child who sees himself as unable to perform must learn to see himself as a capable performer. Your child who is now afraid of the water will later see himself as willing to bathe with parental presence, later to bathe with parental supervision on the shore and still later to swim on his own. Growing up consists of these constant changes, and parents can help children make these transitions. Early independency training aids the child in thinking that he can do the new thing so that he sees himself as competent in the new test. As a result, he develops a realistic self-concept which sees life as a reasonable adventure with new challenges within his grasp and an environment over which he exerts at least partial control.

(12)   Creating is a tender time. Children cannot create when they are constantly fearful or worried, or under undue stress or anxiety. Such children may learn cognitive memory-type production well, but at the expense of a complete "wipeout" of their creative abilities. To be creative, one must be in reasonable mental health, although there are a few notable examples to the contrary. An artist with enormous creative talent may, like Van Gogh, continue creative in spite of mental anguish, but most of us with lesser talents need confidence and good mental health to enable creativity to surface.

Facilitating the Child's Creativity through Mental Health

(1)   Help the child to *value*. A child needs to be valued and to have his ideas valued before he can value others or their ideas. Valuing is a stage in affective learning; previous stages of which are receiving the child and responding to the child. Children need to build their own value system, not take over ours. The values a creative child builds may be divergent ones; he may not wish to emulate his teacher or parent, and this may annoy us. The wise parent concentrates on helping his child to some value system, not necessarily the parent's.

(2)   The child's basic needs in the Maslow hierarchy must be met before he is ready for the task of cognitive self-actualization. If body needs, safety, love, social-ego needs are paramount in a child, he is unready to risk ego capital on creative efforts. The child engrossed in what others think about him, whose place with them is insecure enough to be of concern to him, cannot be creative.

(3)   The child also has to become more comfortable with ambiguity. He must learn to separate it from anxiety. In life there is often more than one answer to a question, and if the question is not well put, there may be no answers at all. The child has to live with this kind of intellectual tension without becoming affectively anxious about it and without aborting the creative ideas which produce it.

(4)   Adult management of socially disapproved behavior also affects the child's concept of himself as a valuable and potentially creative person. Separating the action from the child helps one to be disvalued while the other is not.

(5)   Differentiation of experience is a positive mental health tool which promotes creativity because it clarifies our representation of the world. Parents need to help the young child distinguish between lying and fanciful tales, the older child to discriminate between ends and means, and adolescents to tell the difference between emotions and body feelings.

(6)   In their long march to cultural achievement, creative children pass through many discontinuities with which guidance is concerned. (An example is the change from the small elementary school with one teacher to the large junior high school with its departmentalized classrooms.) Children need enough inner strength at such discontinuity points to see themselves as able to perform in the new setting. If it is expected that children will write, paint, experiment and create in the home, the child is more likely to see his school work as an extension of something which is natural and normal and not a tremendous and new type of task.

(7)   We need to give early rewards for creative behavior. We should make sure that every child's efforts, no matter how poorly executed, bring him enough satisfaction to encourage him to try again. Parents can help by praise rather than criticism. If a child ends up about half right, but with a serious misconception bothering him, we can help by saying, "Well, you made a good try, but I think we can add something else to that," rather than by slapping him down with "That's wrong." We support the process rather than judge the product.

(8)   Creativity is nurtured by easy access to the preconscious; hence, the making of impermissible impulses permissible. To effect this social transformation of the libido, children need help in learning how far to dip into themselves to come up with free-floating ideas,   and they need sympathy, not disapproval, in early and crude attempts to make these ideas socially acceptable.

(9)   Children need help in managing the disappointment and doubt which arise when they have to act alone in some creative endeavor which other people do not understand or to which others may react with derision and ridicule. At such a time the child needs to learn to reward his ego internally in place of the applause he failed to get for initial creative effort, otherwise he may simply turn off the creative thrust entirely. The childish idea of wanting to be first always and perfect always has to be sacrificed to the more realistic concept of a respectable batting average. The creative child may have ten wild ideas while another child has one; sometimes only one of the ten will pay off. If the child is going to be negatively valued for the nine, we will fare poorly. Parents, therefore, must be willing to let children express some of these ideas, and then later help them with some evaluation techniques so that the child realizes that a reasonable pay-off of one good idea for every ten is enough to allow him to be a different, but a helpful, member of society. Ego strength on the part of the child is needed here, but we cannot get creative results with children unless we can help them to grasp this important lesson.

(10)   If parents permit children this reasonable risk-taking behavior, life becomes an adventure in which children can with reasonable effort with reasonable risk, in a world more or less reasonably organized, bring about a result over which they have some control. Again we return to this question: "Am I in control of my environment, or is my environment in control of me?" We want to instill in children the willingness to risk a little where the expectation is large in spite of an occasional failure. This leads to a realistic self-concept with willingness again to risk at a slightly higher level of aspiration. The opposite of this "reasonable risk taking" is that we see in juvenile delinquency, the willingness to risk approval, security, even survival in the face of a blank chance or a long shot with almost certain failure. The creative child thus becomes a "reasonable adventurer" by recognizing that risk taking where one bets on one's abilities in a cognitive way may be a desirable and useful strategy. This is especially true when risk taking becomes a deliberate and realistic choice in which the risk is small compared with the expectation, and not a matter of chance. Children also need help in perfecting risk-taking strategies by identifying finer degrees or categories rather than being satisfied with rougher degrees. (It is harder to diagnose these complex situations, but such intuitive leaps may have heavy cognitive pay-offs.)

Facilitating the Child's Creativity through Social Relationships

Sometimes being creative causes difficulties in the way one relates to other people. Others deride or do not appreciate one's creative efforts, or they give the credit to someone else. Children may need help in "marketing" their creative ideas. Some ways in which parents can help children in this regard are as follows:

(1)   Creative children can be supported in maintaining their creative uniqueness by protecting it from public disapproval. The child needs to know that it is all right to be different from other children, that his parents can respect differences in each other and in his siblings. Parents who illustrate the way to cope with socially caused tensions help their children who have similar problems with which to cope.

(2)   Peer sanctions against being creative and "different" are often very hard for children to cope with. As a result, they may "turn off" their creativity rather than to run the risk of losing friends. Parents need to talk with children at times like these, and perhaps intervene, by helping them find new peers who can or will appreciate their differences as valuable.

(3)   Whenever a child is proving creative about being naughty or devious, it is usually because he has not enough responsibility and needs more. We may need to help children discriminate between constructive rather than destructive nonconformity. The difference is situational in the first instance but compulsive in the second. Nonconformity in the first instance is a response to unreasonable unintelligent adult demands; in the second case, it may become a compulsive, destructive reaction to any demands at all.

(4)   A child's mind has been compared to a "twin fountain of creativity and destructiveness." The more we open the creative fountain, the more we tend

to close the destructive one. The child who is denied constructive outlets may turn to becoming creatively devious in getting his way.

(5) We should not shirk from making the complicated explanation when it is called for or portraying nature as complex rather than simple. We can also help children refine questioning, and suggest modifications of the search approach when there seems to be no answer to a particular line of questioning. Very often a child's questions reveal misconceptions or inaccurate facts. The four-year-old who asks his mother "Why aren't these rockets likely to shoot down God?" needs help in rethinking and rephrasing his concept.

(6) Not all learning needs to be evaluated. A good athletic coach has practice most of the time and only evaluates during scrimmage or games. Some adults, however, act as if a child is always in a game for keeps. Creative response is stultified or blocked when evaluation occurs too quickly or too often. We need to make clear to children that there will be times when they are not being evaluated. Effective students learn that they are not making mistakes when they are practicing. They may be discovering different or invalid answers, but they are narrowing down the remaining possibilities.

(7) A child's curiosity and questioning should always be respected. Sometimes children will question peers or adults and will be turned off as a result of ignorance or embarrassment. Parents can help restore the child's curiosity which has received social disapproval by trying to answer the question as honestly and fully as possible.

(8) Creative children are self-starters with lots of energy, a high degree of independence and a great deal of initiative. These characteristics can be hindered by too much supervision; however, when a child starts on something, we should encourage him to go through with it. On the other hand, if a child persists, or eagerly reaches for new alternatives, it is best to let him go and give him his "head." Parents sometimes ask: "Shall I let him read; he's only three?" Why not? Other mothers will query: "Shall I let him take all those adult books out of the library?" Why shouldn't he? Have you ever been hurt by a book you wanted to read? Interest should never be denied or learning withheld from children.

(9) Parents can take a leaf of the book from developments in the educational world with regard to values and social behavior. In the past, these areas became involved with religious or moral codes. But the concept of values, interests and attitudes can be dealt with by the parent or teacher in terms of the Krathwohl and Bloom (1965) "affective domain of educational objectives." The process of receiving, responding and valuing is a significant part of learning to feel our social responsibilities about things, events and persons. We can help children in this dimension by receiving information tolerantly, showing attention when new information comes to us (even if it is "rock and roll" music), valuing it, then helping to set the value into its proper perspective. For example, parents can help youngsters evaluate and put in proper place good television programs over poor ones, good comic books over poor ones, and so on. This concept of setting taste and values for youngsters is as easy as that, and these examples are a good place in which to start.

The writer can remember coming to agreement with his adolescent daughter some years ago that at least one of the ways she could tell a "B" movie from an "A" movie was that, in a "B" movie, she would know what was going to happen next. This is a very simple kind of awareness, but it is one of the entering wedges in helping a child look at something and say "Is this good?" instead of just taking it in as raw experience.

(10) New and challenging facts must be talked over, processed and digested to become concepts out of which children can form some meaningful view of the world. Finding related meanings in life is the real process of discovering values and is necessary for a productive and satisfying life. Creative children may develop a different set from our own, but if we can help the child digest the experience, we essentially mediate it; and the value emerging, while the child's and not ours, is still something we have helped to develop.

The child needs to discover through home discussion that people, even loved ones, perceive the same situation differently, that there is often more than one answer to a question or more than one method of procedure. Children are fortunate who live in a home where differences and new ideas are accepted and not just tolerated. Such children soon find out that it is all right to differ with people, that you can still respect and love them, whether they are your playmates, parents or other adults. In fact, they discover the goodness of individual differences.

TEACHER AND COUNSELOR STIMULATION

How can the professional educator help the child become more creative? As education has become more aware of and interested in creativity, it has become more obvious that the development and maintenance of creativity is not purely an outgrowth of curriculum experiences but of teacher-student and counselor-student interrelationships and attitudes. The guidance staff is responsible for not only encouraging and ensuring the orientation of learning to creativity, but for a classroom and school climate which will foster it. Studies of the personality of the creative child (Torrance, 1962, 1964) clarify many aspects which can be promoted by the teaching and by the guidance staff.

(1) *The creative child is often physically and socially mature for his age, intelligently aware of his environment and his own needs and abilities, fully functioning and responsible.* In this respect, he is opposite of the personality of the delinquent or to the student hampered by a resistant or maladaptive attitude. Dr. Paul Torrance, upon being asked by the writer "What makes a child creative?" replied: "Anything that makes him more alive." A zest for life and exuberance of mental and physical health is often evident in bright creative children. Whatever guidance programs can do to help every child to better mental health and maturity will aid whatever creativity he may possess.

All children have some elements of creativity as a result of their mental health. Guidance personnel has the responsibility that the school climate, personalization of relationships, and elements of curriculum preserve, maintain and foster this mental health for all. The children may not become notably creative, but they will become more productive and less vulnerable to mental illness. Conversely, the identification of children with special potential for creativity is also a most important guidance function.

In this advocacy of more complete guidance services, we do not imply that the guidance program can produce creativity, but only that it will tend to bring out or make manifest latent creativity of children. Most educational stimulation for children merely preserves and develops their creative performance rather than producing it. Children are naturally creative and only require the right atmosphere to manifest it.

(2) *Creative thinking takes place only when more essential need systems have been satisfied.* A child's physiological and biological needs come before the onset of intellectual and personal self-actualization. Body needs, safety, love and self-esteem must be satisfied before the child can risk ego-capital on creative ventures. Counselors need to help their children manage their social and personal anxieties enough to be creative.

(3) *The process of creative performance is similar to "mining ore" from the preconscious.* Many children are reluctant to mine this lode because of the frightening or unpleasant things which may be discovered. These scary, uncanny memories and experiences are part of the Sullivanian "not me" (1952), disassociated frightening fragments which are part of the preconscious. In the mansion of our intellect we all have a room, attic or closet we never show to others which consists of assorted junk piled up from bygone days. Like a toymaker's attic, it is often filled with severed heads, limbs and torsos of the dolls we somehow failed to put together. The problem the child has is to avoid panic when he goes into the attic, develop the confidence to bring back the latent ideas from their preconscious resting places, develop the patience to examine the idea carefully and finally to keep the mind tranquil enough so that this whole process of inner exploration can take place. The ore comes out in unpolished form, and the dolls come down with their heads on backwards, and the child may easily reject an idea which, with more attention and polishing, would show real worth. Acceptance and understanding without premature evaluation encourage the experience and continuation of creativity. The child can best effect suspension of evaluation himself when in the presence of a supportive, nondirective person, such as the counselor.

(4) *Adults can promote the process by which children channel their creative thrust and aggressiveness into constructive and not destructive channels.* Creative children are going to be nonconformists. We can help them to become constructive rather than destructive nonconformists. The difference is often subtle and imperceptible to adult eyes. But, whereas the constructive nonconformist is situational and selective in his attack of society and its ills (as Thoreau was over the Mexican War), the nonconstructive nonconformist is compulsive and nondiscriminating in attacking everybody and everything (as in "trashing" buildings). Creative children are ambivalent toward creativity destructiveness and may create and destroy practically in the same breath. We need to help them separate these functions so that in the positive or creative systole, they

channel their energy into constructive action and in the negative diastole, into harmless dissipation of energy (such as thrashing around and making splashes in a swimming pool). In the beginning, like all children, creative children do not distinguish much between being creative and being destructive. If the creative actions are not more rewarded than the destructive ones, it will be difficult later to untangle the child's ambivalence in this area.

(5) *Counselors and other adults need to provide support for children to participate in creative experiences.* Creative experiences are peak experiences, and they require a focusing and constricting of attention so that a new perspective emerges. Psychological courage to give of oneself, to withstand a sense of awe or strangeness, to conserve curiosity in the face of scary novelty is required. Just as oxygen may be required by the extended perspiring athlete as well as by the expiring invalid, so generous amounts of counseling may be necessary at the time of creativity as well as at the removal of psychopathology. A young girl going out on a date needs to be groomed to establish her self-confidence in meeting this exciting but strange new boy. We have discovered in our summer workshop for children that they also need "grooming" by the counselor before class to "set" them for creative endeavor. This often consists of support, admiration and confidence expressed by the counselor in the child.

(6) *Many times the creative child will find himself alone, neglected or unrewarded as a result of his creative response.* His peers and adult acquaintances will not appreciate or even notice some of his creative actions and at other times they will strongly oppose them. Many creative children have their ideas turned down without examination because their manner or approach provokes opposition; the same idea may later be advocated by a more popular or respected group member, and it will be readily adopted or rewarded. When this happens, creative children may become embittered and wish to withdraw from the group, or they will "reform" and conform for the sake of external approval. The counselor, in talking to the child at this point, can indicate that such steps deny the child's creative gifts. The child must learn to reward his own efforts and to market his different ideas. Benjamin Franklin's *Autobiography* contains a famous and helpful recital of his early difficulties in this regard and the ways he found to overcome them. The counselor may not always be able to improve the external situation, but he can aid the child in understanding the internal one; namely, his own feelings and appreciation for his own efforts.

(7) *Guidance for the creative child involves not only the solving of problems but a positive counseling promoting mental health.* Significant for all students, guidance is vital for creative ones. In our summer institute for promoting creativity in gifted children, we found that gifted children willingly sought and absorbed the counselors' efforts of a one to twenty-five counselor-client ratio, which is twelve times the concentration of guidance services often recommended. To deal with more complex problems, to bring into focus a variety of abilities in longer process sequences (for more constructive endeavors with less possibility of external reward), the creative youth needs more mental health than the average. He needs it to handle without disabling stress and to tolerate the

prolonged problems, which he must solve alone, and the solutions, which only he can find. Like a diver whose oxygen supply enables him to stay longer under water, he must be better equipped for the strange conditions under which he must labor. We enhance the creativity of those who are highly able cognitively by helping them to become highly sound emotionally.

Establishing the Creativity Cycle and Managing Its Depressed Phase

The process of creativity is a cycle very much like that of a heat pump. The latter (in the cooling mode) focuses a supply of cold air into the interior of the refrigerator and dissipates the hot exhaust air into the room. There is a similar cycle in creative action; first, a positive wave of creative production followed by a down phase of essentially negative emotions, often depression. The phenomenon of "post partum" depression as a biological effect is well known, but it also occurs in creative process, where there is less knowledge concerning its etiology. Depression after childbirth is not rare among women, and a similar, although less severe, depression after coitus is common in men. This effect is not always present, especially in those of robust health. An analogy seems to exist in persons who are mentally rather than physically creative, such as artists, writers, musicians, actors, composers. It also seems to occur after creative but more mundane events such as hosting a party, helping a client in psychotherapy, making a speech, etc. It is also found in adolescent students after some of their more exciting incidents.

At such a time there is the feeling that the best has gone out of one. The term "spent," which also applies to the physical situation, is apposite. One feels "used up"; muscle tone is flaccid and slack; one doubts anything else can be attempted; there may even be a death wish, or a desire to punish oneself. What can the counselor do to help the creative youth in this depressed phase of the creativity cycle? A number of suggestions may be appropriate:

(1) An understanding of the previous rationale may itself help the youth who comes to see this as a part of the normal, not a pathological, process. An important characteristic of cyclic or periodic processes is certain change, and frequently the availability of help is itself therapeutic.

(2) It is important to realize that descents from peak experiences (and creativity is a peak experience) are apt to be disappointing. The frustration at the loss of pleasure is frequently associated with the appearance of certain types of brain waves as the individual vainly tries to maintain the pleasurable level. Change or disturbance of an anticipated level of positive reinforcement is always distasteful. Moodiness reflects the interim method the ego uses to accommodate to this loss of pleasure without an outburst of hostility.

(3) The creative youth needs assurance that creativity is not limited or completely spent, once used. On the contrary, like a well which soon refills when water is dipped from it, creativity, like most other powers, improves when full functioning and actualized.

(4)   The creative youth should be informed that, while a pause and rest after creative effort is natural and normal, it need not be a source of depression. The negative cycle can be dissipated in harmless ways or in recreation. As part of the natural rhythm, it can be as refreshing as sleep after physical love.

(5)   The creative youth should be aware that some depression may be felt when the creative product is not immediately appreciated by others. The youth may have expected extrinsic rewards from society, not realizing the joys of intrinsic reward. It is in action not accolade where we come to terms with our identity in full functioning.

(6)   Creative youth needs personal evaluation and love after its exertions. Those close to creative youth should give it this support during and following the time of creation. Otherwise the ego is thrown back on self-reward and may become a prey to depression on the down cycle. Therapeutic aids to creative persons during and after creative performance act like vitamins for a prospective mother to prevent the "post partum" depression which may follow. The amplitude of the mood swingings which have exalted the creative individual into the heights may in turn plunge him into despair; this "dark valley" is a very real locale for many of us. Often there has been implanted in the psyche during the initiative period the idea that one must pay for outbursts of joy and energy with remorse and guilt immobilization. But creative persons need not develop these patterns any more than mothers need suffer "post partum" depression. The remedy for both is a matter of good mental and physical health plus understanding of the situation and getting rid of one's psychological hang-ups. Some youth, who might otherwise become creative, stifle or deflect its creative thrust because of the resulting guilt; others feel too inhibited to use their full initiative in a joyful venturing forth. In any case, the world as well as the individual is the loser.

Children are especially helped to preserve creativity by nonauthoritarian attitudes on the part of educators who avoid early and negative evaluations of the child's efforts. The child must first be the recipient of, so that he may later become the producer of, constructive rather than pejorative evaluations if he is to persist in creativity. Creative fantasy becomes bonded to reality in this manner. Teachers have a powerful impact upon the child's opportunities for success and the extent to which he can win prestige from peers. The teacher selects the type of evaluation the child faces and provides the climate which encourages or discourages intellectual risk taking. Teachers may subtly discourage children's search for creativity by limiting opportunities and activities which stimulate divergent thinking by emphasis on tight control and teacher prestige. As a result, the child may fear to make any intuitive response that threatens the teacher in any way or causes the child to lose irretrievable status. The teacher also discourages creativity when only the child's convergent thinking is recognized, or rewarded, when memory processes are emphasized, when anxiety is aggravated, when the text, rather than the children's thoughts and ideas, becomes the only authority.

There is a tendency for the conventional teacher to teach the simpler skills of cognition and memory to the detriment of stimulating the more complex aspects of the structure of intellect. Since the divergent thinking slab is well up this complexity scale, as are transformations and implications in the products classification, stereotyped teaching to somewhat anxious children tends to wash out the more creative aspects of the curriculum while preserving the rote learnings. Such a classroom may appear letter perfect on a cognitive memory test and yet have all creative potential of the children smothered by the teaching method employed.

ENVIRONMENTAL STIMULATION OF YOUTH IN UNIVERSITIES

When a person of the required degree of mental ability and mental health is stimulated by the environment, creative production results. This outcome may be shown in theorem form:

Creativity = (mental health) (natural ability) (stimulation).

As the process of development escalates from biological drives to social relationships, creativity, which begins almost naturally for the child, must now be more heavily reinforced by environmental stimulation. The developmental process, which almost automatically reinforced creativity at the start, is no longer sufficient and must be assisted by educational stimulation which now becomes essential and crucial for further escalation.

An important function of higher education is to ameliorate the incipient authoritarianism of youth revealed by the dependence on group norms or "other directedness" so characteristic of the identity period. This ethocentrism is effectively negated by the development of personal autonomy during the intimacy period, thus preventing the kind of nightmare graphically described by Erich Fromm in *Escape from Freedom.* Without this kind of stimulation to think for himself, the young person succumbs to group domination and direction in contrast to the inner directedness of the intelligent democrat. The focus of higher education in this country, then, should be oriented toward helping youth meet the last of Havighurst's developmental tasks—intellectual-moral adjustment.

The function of the university, therefore, is not so much to intellectualize youth as to socialize them and to make them humane enough to be participant electors in a true democracy. In such countries as Latin America and Greece, where higher education has failed this task, one finds an upper class with fascistic tendencies and lack of concern for those less fortunate in their society. The result is to prevent the development of what William Graham Sumner once called the two fundamental attributes of a democracy: concern for the governed by the governors and an open road to the top for talent no matter where it may be found. The closing of the "open society" results in some form of totalitarianism, and the danger to our society is only too clear. This is why the universities are such present foci of political action. The key aspect of university stimulation is *autonomy* because it inhibits dependence on authority and allows for the preservation of the creative function.

This is not the place to make full recommendations regarding desirable changes in university governance, but a few representative innovations are presented:

(1)   Creativity should itself become the focus of a university course in which students are given instruction in the development and use of their creative powers. Material, well adapted for this purpose, is the Osborn Parnes method of creative problem solving, now being used on a trial basis in four lower division courses at the State University College at Buffalo.

(2)   Since positive mental health contributes to creativity, the university counseling services should reach those students needing individual or group guidance. The role of group guidance in the maintenance of positive mental health, rather than its use in psychotherapy, should be further explored.

(3)   The unacknowledged and often unrecognized "press" of a particular university toward implicit objectives, which are not part of its catalog statement, needs careful investigation. These presses are sustained by an unofficial system of rewards and punishments and may involve conformity, nonconformity, fraternity life, big time athletics, or what have you. Often this press is at variance with student needs or mental health principles. Work done by Heist at Berkeley and Katz (1969) at Stanford clearly indicates that in actuality this divergence is considerable and is a significant cause of student apathy and unrest.

(4)   The university should recognize its responsibility for socialization rather than just intellectualization of students and for the development of autonomy rather than conformity. Unfortunately, the major emphasis is sometimes the opposite. The nature of such university change has been documented by Chickering (1969) who concluded that "Development occurs through cycles of differentiation and integration."

(5)   The routine administrative procedures necessary in a large university create apathy and boredom. Students justly feel that they have been dehumanized and that their personalities are replaced by an IBM number. These practices tend to prevent the person-to-person relationships between faculty and students which are so necessary for creative learning. The Knapp and Goodrich studies of the 1950s showed clearly that small, midwestern-type colleges were far more productive of future scientists than large, prestigious universities. Contacts with faculty in small classes were at a maximum in these institutions, and the personal element appeared to be the salient factor involved. Hopefully, some way can be devised whereby human contact may be maintained through the creation of small colleges within larger universities.

(6)   The quality of academic instruction at most universities is deplorably low. More innovative methods than the lecture-recitation can certainly be found. Faculties have been notoriously lax concerning innovation and renewal in curriculum and teaching methods. It has been assumed that every Ph.D., indeed, every graduate student, knows how to teach. More effort by the faculty to reform curriculum and teaching methods, fueled by a relaxation on the press for promotion through research only, plus bonuses paid to outstanding teachers would have a

helpful effect. Above all, the process of education at the university level should be that of discovery, not subjection to rote memory processes.

(7)   There are perhaps too many students attending American universities for the wrong reasons. Some may be there for the prestige, social life, athletics or contacts the university provides. Because it is probably not feasible to bar or remove them, it may be more appropriate to provide honors classes involving creative methods for those who are able and who want to pursue the larger aspects of a liberal or professional education.

(8)   University administrators, trustees and alumni as well as the surrounding community have tended to regard a university as a source of good athletes and sports entertainment. A school primarily involved in big-time football cannot pay sufficient attention to the real functions of an institution of higher education. This recommendation requires change on the part of the alumni and the community served by the university.

(9)   If an authoritarian church group should attempt to intimidate the professors at a modern university by forbidding them to teach evolution, for example, there would be a dreadful outcry that academic freedom was being imperiled. Yet academic freedom is equally imperiled when any other group, either inside or outside the university, attempts to dictate what shall or what shall not be taught and in what manner. All attempt to politicize or in any other way put pressure on university professors should be resisted at all costs, no matter how worthy the cause may seem at the time.

(10)   Universities cannot promote creativity unless they can prosper rather than merely survive. In a period of rising prices, when the public and patrons of a university withhold its receipts or tax monies, these persons are effectively contributing toward stifling creativity and innovation within its walls. In the long run, the public and the alumni will get the kind of university for which they are willing to pay. Creativity is one of the first casualties of a strained budget.

(11)   It is time that universities paid attention to the commentary and social criticism offered by Reich (1970) in *The Greening of America*. The development of Consciousness III, which is inner directed and an integral part of the existential *Eigenwelt* should be aided and not opposed by the press of the institution. This type of social conscience, which stands for individuality in the face of inroads on freedom by the corporate state, has a pedigree as far back as Thoreau and Jefferson. Changes are bound to come, and it is much better if they are mediated by universities in an atmosphere of reason and understanding than if they are provoked into violent upheaval by rigid and encrusted institutions. In stating that our young people are capable of developing into a new level of consciousness, Reich seems to have reached a sociological statement of a thesis which we have attempted to develop from a psychological viewpoint. The central, unifying factor is creative, and innovative functioning and a new level of consciousness. These processes are certainly in the mainstream of educational effort and, hence, part of the responsibility of the university to promote and foster.

ADULT STIMULATION, ESPECIALLY TRAVEL

The tendency to regress into conservative and authoritarian views is not confined to adolescence. It is unfortunately a phenomenon found at every instance of stasis in human life. Thus older people, fearful and unaccustomed to change, easily drift to the Right for, as the late humorist Thurber is supposed to have remarked, "It takes a bright man to distinguish his own dissolution from that of the human race." Some individuals continue at the university or other intellectual pursuits; for most others, travel, particularly foreign travel, is their best mode of education.

Foreign travel has several results. First it jars the individual out of his encrusted customs. He must perforce adapt or adjust to new habits and routines of washing, eating, sleeping, speaking and other aspects of daily living. He finds that a different language does not translate exactly, so that there are subtle meanings which cannot be conveyed adequately in his own idiom. He realizes with a start that people of different cultures react differently to those events whose psychological responses are controlled by the limbic region of the brain—those conditions which arouse fear, fight, flight or the more tender passions. One of the most remarkable things for the traveler to notice is the very different perceptions of danger held by different cultures. Poisonous snakes, wild animals, smog, the common cold, police violence, racial strife, pollution, illness, overhead high-tension wires, unprotected culverts, unguarded railway crossings and highway hazards are all situations which are considered especially dangerous in some cultures and completely commonplace in others.

Travel is stimulating in shaking up ideas and perceptions precisely because different cultures perceive differently those situations which involve emotions (particularly those of danger), risk, hostility, insults, sex, fear, dread, loathing and all the other aspects of the Sullivanian "bad me" and "not me." These affective differences are initially extremely attention getting because of their shock value. (What American "skinny dipping" for the first time in a Japanese bath has not had this cultural difference brought to his attention more forcefully, for example, than being reminded of the conceptual difference between the Romance language use of the conditional and our future indicative?) Cultural shocks are precisely that; hence their potential for new insight about ourselves.

The next stage is for the traveler to discover good things and processes in the other culture. Recovering from his culture shock, he begins to realize that there are logical and practical reasons for the way things are done in the strange environment, and some of these might be just as good or better than the way things are done at home.

This leads to a further stage where the traveler quietly begins to reexamine a number of habitual practices and customs which he had considered sacrosanct. For example, why is it that Americans pay such idolatrous respect to our flag, when other peoples do not have a similar attachment to theirs? Why is our society so "hipped" on guns, when they are banned or regarded as extremely dangerous in most other cultures? The writer will never forget the pained insight which came upon him when a gentle questioner from New Zealand asked rather plaintively: "With all that water in Southern California why don't you share some with Tijuana?"

The realization that some ideas, customs and beliefs considered sacred, or as applying throughout space and time, are actually only valid or true within our frame of reference is an extremely liberating one for the traveler. It helps him for the first time to get outside his cultural ethos and, like a fish who jumps out of water, to find out more about the medium in which he has been immersed and which he took for granted. In other words, it helps us separate the signal from the static, the figure from the background.

Several results follow from this reorganization of concepts: First, there is a feeding in of alternative suggestions which increase the flexibilities of the traveler's thinking. No more is he at the mercy of his cultural constructs; he can now see around and behind them.

Secondly, new ways of doing things are powerful suggestors of verbal or other analogies, generalizations or applications which can be taken back to the old culture. Trading goods between different countries has always been a profitable business; trading ideas is even more profitable.

If environmental stimulation is essential to adult creativity, one may with propriety ask "What are the mechanisms by which the stimulation accomplishes the act?" While no doubt some aspects of creative response come from the unusualness of the environment, which depart from custom, it may be suggested that it may operate in the following straightforward manner:

A differential cultural stimulus suggests a parallelism of an old ratio or relationship, much in the manner of a semantic verbal analog. Consider, for example, the following table:

	(S) greater	(P) lesser
nations	Spain	Portugal
elements	sodium	potassium

One has known about the relationship between sodium and potassium since high school days (the relationship is implicit; one does not have to verbalize it.) Then one travels on the Iberian Peninsula, and one connects Spain and Portugal in the same way. The common element is greater to lesser, or S to P, and this is where the creative link comes in. Travel has here suggested a generalization of an old ratio which transforms the matrix from elements to nations. This is, to be sure, a trivial example; but a great deal of scientific creativity suggests in similar bridging by means of a semantic verbal analog (or a proportion in mathematical terms) the gulf between two unique systems. The literary name for this is metaphor or simile, and it is also a favorite of poets.

We have seen before how play is particularly helpful in reorienting the ego to reality and also useful for the child in reducing pressures enough to allow him through daydreams or fantasy some relaxation of the compartmentalization between the ego and the preconscious.

There are two primary forms of adult play—sexual activity and travel. Sexual activity, while sometimes productive of inspiration, tends to be deficient in new stimulus percepts and to drain off energy. Travel, on the other hand, subjects adults to vastly increased amounts of new stimuli, much of it (if the trip is outside the native culture) of particularly novel and striking proportions. It also forces cognition or "shaking up" of previously fixed ideas and, hence, makes for creative response.

Of adult prerequisites to creativity, certainly environmental stimulation and an open life style are the most important. It may be desirable again to point out that these two components do not suddenly become vital; it is rather that they are gradually more emphasized as biological development is completed. The slowing down of developmental process in the physical sense needs to be accompanied by a speeding up of developmental process in the social sense if creative production is to be sustained. Of all the varieties of environmental stimulation, education is certainly the most important, with travel a close second.

Withdrawal and return. We have spoken of creativity-destructivity as a cycle which has to be stabilized. One can also look at the cycle as one of withdrawal-return. Most of us are loath, once having tasted the pleasures of return, to again brave the hazards and deprivations of withdrawal. But to evoke creative response, we must complete the cycle on occasion and engage in a rather continuous application of it.

It is as if one gains creative power from the change in attitude in withdrawal and return much as an electric generator develops current flow from the changing attitude of the armature as it cuts across lines of magnetic force. For the armature to remain stationary and preserve the same attitude will not do; neither will it do if there is no magnetic field. The generation of electric power is thus an exact analog of the generation of creative ideas.

We, therefore, need on a periodic basis repeatedly to put ourselves into the complementary attitudes of withdrawal and return. For those of us unused to meditation or to artistic absorption, only travel and the gross interruption of our regular routine will suffice. For travel forces us out of our routines, makes us withdraw from the daily round and strips our lives of encrusted preconceptions. Travel is thus the withdrawal of the active man.

Transcendence of cultural background. The final development task of the superior adult is transcendence of his cultural background. In this process, the individual breaks out of his cultural milieu as he has previously broken out of his egocentric and familial matrices, moving into greater freedom each time. The cultural envelope, that last protective skin enveloping the individual and both protecting him and keeping him from experiencing and making sense out of reality, is no longer necessary for he is now mature enough to operate independently of his environment.

Unlocking of the chrysalis, formerly a necessary protection but now a fetter to flight and freedom, is always sensed by less developed individuals in the culture as a dangerous and threatening alteration. Thus Jesus was reviled for breaking the Sabbath, Gandhi ostracized for violating caste taboos with the untouchables and Roosevelt characterized as a "traitor to his class" when he urged legislation conferring benefits on the unemployed. Similar disapproval is imposed on others who unloosen conventional taboos. While necessary for those still bound to Bagehot's "cake of custom," such prohibitions become unnecessary for the fully actualized individual who is now able to operate without restrictions in the unobstructed world.

Travel outside the cultural milieu is valuable in producing the environmental stimulation necessary to accomplish the transformation. "How are you going to keep them down on the farm, once they have seen Paris?" went the old refrain. Thus a J. P. Marquand hero who travels outside New England can never return to it again psychologically or feel the same allegiance to its customs and taboos, though he may dutifully make the geographical pilgrimage back to his homeland.

Transcendence of the culture does not mean a disregard for all aspects of it but an ecumenicalism which attempts to bring what is best in the culture into a larger synthesis. The highest ethical aspects especially remain relevant and are, as it were, distilled and appear as an essence. Thus Jesus proclaims that the Sabbath is made for man and not man for the Sabbath, while Gandhi rewrote the Hindu scripture "christianizing" it. In every case the cultural background, having served as a matrix, is sloughed off, and the individual, now developed to complete freedom, even freedom from his cultural past, can now become fully functioning and integral as a human being in the world at large.

FOETALIZATION

In previous sections, the forces of environmental stimulation playing on the life span of the individual man which advance his creative powers have been scrutinized. We should not leave this chapter without a discussion of the manner in which evolution has accomplished a similar task for the human species.

Man represents a unique combination of an animal base and a consciousness which soars to the stars. Nature produced him by a process which Bolk (1926) called the "foetalization of the ape." This involved an enlargement of the immature phase of primate development and its more prominent emphasis in the life span which made possible new and increased opportunities for complex learning and experience. Foetalization in man, then, describes a stretching out of the docile learning period into a larger proportion of the whole life span. During this plastic dependency and apprenticeship, mammalian family life and play extended conditioning and more complex learnings into developmental changes which transformed the primate into a human being. (See figure 8.)

In all humans, this lengthened span of immaturity which reaches into the first three decades is devoted to learning and education, and hopefully to creative performance, before man becomes in senility more like an old ape—taciturn, solitary, hairy and immobile. Through foetalization, evolution provides opportunity for man to develop a creative mind before he degenerates into a reactive apish-like creature. Man, of course, does not become an ape, but without stimulation of his higher faculties, he, too, may experience premature senility (like the ape at an earlier age).

Human beings often feel that they are the final and perfect product of evolution, which has somehow ceased with the production of this masterpiece. There is no reason to believe, however, that the forces of evolution are no longer in operation. Evidence of this continuation may be seen in differences between superior and more average individuals in any society, for the life style of the

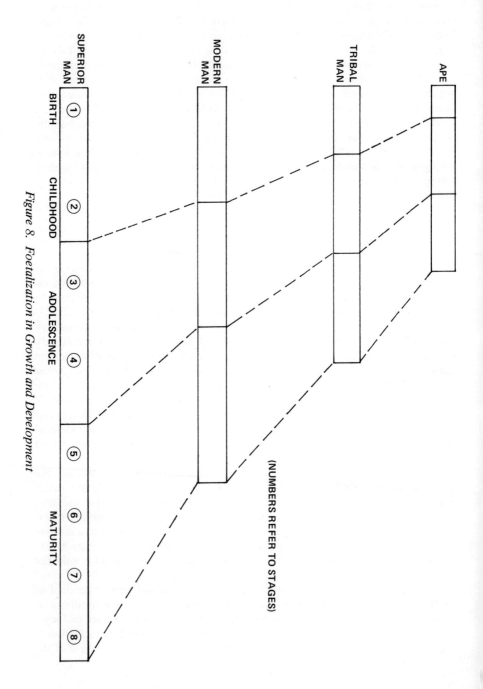

Figure 8. *Foetalization in Growth and Development*

superior individual points the directional thrust of evolutionary progress for all mankind. Nature seems to have granted superior youth a little more time in the foetalization process and to have placed more emphasis on this period. In consequence, such fortunate individuals tend to have a youthful aspect, even in maturity.

Furthermore, bright young males go through a process of continued foetalization which makes them appear younger and less mature (viewed in relation to their own ultimate growth and attainments) than more average youth. The Kinsey and Pomeroy study (1948) was one of the first to report this in regard to differential sexual practices, but such differences may well extend to other aspects of human behavior.

This book, as we have said in the preface, discusses developmental processes leading to creativity in males. (The reason for leaving out female development is ignorance on our part, not prejudice.) The developmental process in males is perforce a development toward maleness or psychological masculinity. Hence a counterprocess of foetalization which invokes delay or prolongation in maturing appears relatively like feminization. This is not a homosexual deviation, nor is it abnormal nor effeminate. It represents a slowing down of development (which is not arrest) but which gives added emphasis to a particular period, much as a conductor would slow down the tempo of an orchestra in a compelling musical passage. Foetalization partakes more of developmental latency than arrest because it refers to a longer period of growth in the life span and to more absorption in extended cognitive experiences, rather than the immediate tasks of adult sexuality, and, finally, because it is not a *decalage* or cultural lag but an evolutionary change.

The cultural and, hence, psychological stereotypes of masculinity and femininity (as measured on psychological tests) are only remotely related to biological sexual roles, being mainly reinforced from cultural values. In the past, these have been restrictive of the full human development of both men and women, assigning to each certain set tasks and prohibiting others (women may not aggress; men may not cry). The repressions of emotionality, spontaneity and esthetic responsiveness have been as crippling to the creative development of men as the restrictions on drive, mastery and zest in achievement have retarded the full development of women. Psychology is now recognizing that the human attributes of mental health and personality, particularly in superior adults, overlap the sex roles. A personality like Gandhi had an almost "feminine" mothering quality, while Eleanor Roosevelt had a certain masculine dash. But these self-actualized individuals did not achieve mastery of their productive potentialities at the expense of their true sexuality.[1]

Nature has also favored the superior youth by giving him more "peak" to shoot at. In other words, because of the increased range of development for him, he is longer in the process of getting there, and being longer in process, he reaps the multiple benefits of that process. A third advantage results from individual efforts made by persons themselves, while in process of growth, to create new experiences and responses, preventing them from a premature

---

[1] The major ideas of this paragraph are those of Sybil Richardson.

atrophy into an unself-actualized old age. These efforts are interactions with the environment and are not concerned (as are the previous) with hereditary or genotypic characteristics.

Perhaps it is desirable again to emphasize that foetalization is not feminization, but a process of slowing up of aging in superior males. It does not refer to effeminacy or to homosexuality. Superior male adults evidence a youthful quality which preserves their verbal ability, creative power and dynamic process. John F. Kennedy represents a good example of this process which gave him a youthful vitality when he was actually in middle age. He is also a good example of male heterosexuality.

It is possible that W. T. Sheldon came as near as anyone to identifying this quality when he talked about the "t-component" (1949, p. 21). He calls it "the component of thorobredness" or the "the physical quality of the animal," and he distinguishes it from gynandromorphy (or having a female type figure). This index of "tissue fineness" has a psychological correlate in the "occupational level" scale of the *Strong Vocational Interest Blank*. Males high in intelligence or the professions tend to show feminine interests (and females show the opposite). Indeed Walberg (1969), in a study entitled *Physics, Femininity and Creativity*, traces the interesting relationship between these variables.

Schneider (1950, p. 135) describes one of the creative dynamos of the artist as a

> . . . heightened bisexuality, as a psychic counterpart of the third identification which we have tried to describe as stemming from the gifted child's capacity for greater relationships in his identifying process.[1]

It is this greater ability to relate which appears to be the source of pioneering and originality in artistic and verbal creation.

Other examples of this "foetalization" effect which gives a facade of femininity and youthful appearance in great men would include Michelangelo, Da Vinci, Goethe, Shelley, Keats, Wordsworth, Thoreau, Whitman, F. D. Roosevelt and many others.

We should note that generally the issue is not sexuality but relationship to the father figure. A particularly strong stimulus to creativity comes when the youth feels it necessary and possible to go beyond his father's accomplishments and "make up for" the failure of his father to reach desired objectives.

Miller's *Death of a Salesman* is a powerful dramatic treatment of failure of a son to make this adjustment. Schneider (1950, p. 251), in analyzing the play, states that: "A society which destroys fatherhood makes criminals out of its sons." It is precisely the impulse to become nondestructive (and, therefore, creative) that leads the uncommon youth to try to redeem his father.

Stitesville (1967, p. 3551), in doctoral research reviewing life history patterns of highly creative inventors, made the following summary:

---

[1]From page 135, Daniel E. Schneider, *The Psychoanalyst and The Artist*, Copyright, 1950, Farrar, Straus and Giroux. Used by permission.

The pattern is: "By my clever solutions to other's problems I shall win applause." The applause is viewed as self-validation, approval and acceptance by the rest of humanity. . . . Inventor's fathers were often frustrated inventors or engineers. The sons appear to live a life in which they redeem the father. They do for him what he himself was unable to accomplish.

We know that the relationship between an abnormal (XYY) chromosome male and the average (XY) male is that the latter compared with the former is brighter, more docile, more social and less destructive. Can we not extrapolate that the relationship between the average male and the superior individual is at least a small continuance of the same process, so that the latter becomes brighter, more docile, more social and less destructive (more creative)?

Indeed, it is remarkable that in many creative men, one finds a conscious attempt to explore "feminine" interests and to gain the "balance" and "receptivity" which psychological femininity adds to the individual's powers. Interestingly enough, no less a person than Erikson studies this very facet in the heroic life of Gandhi (1969). Gandhi, as revealed by Erikson's psychoanalytic biography deliberately sought to "mother" his parents and early in life to assume nurturance of others. This in-depth analysis of a modern saint makes fascinating reading because of its uncovering of the developmental process and the conscious effort at feminization in Gandhi's life. (Our cultural values force us to regard this process as "feminization," but actually full paternity in the generativity stage involves nurturance, "succorance" and other gentle virtues toward one's children which are undervalued or underemphasized in our violence-prone culture so that we regard expression of them as somehow "feminine.")

Some aspects of Gandhi's childhood and parental relations, as revealed by Erikson, provide a picture of a bright, precocious and creative child who early assumed a protective relationship toward others. Especially significant to Erikson are Gandhi's relationships with his mother and father. The close mother-son bond, often seen in creative men, is found here, but the specific trend in Gandhi's life appears to have evolved out of his special attachment-ambivalence toward his father whom, Erikson suggests, Gandhi sought to "redeem."

Surely this process, for which we have used the somewhat inappropriate words "foetalization" and "feminization" (because no better ones exist), is far more a positive integration and summation of both sexual roles rather than a regression toward effeminacy or homosexuality. It is seen in the peculiar and concomitant relationships which such men have with their fathers—as that of equal. It is as if they wish to become their own fathers or to redeem the father. Thus Erikson says of Gandhi (1969, p. 102):

The child is the father of the man makes new, special and particular sense for special men; they indeed have (i.e.) *become their own fathers*, and in a way their father's fathers while not yet adult.

Again he remarks of Gandhi's relations to his son (1969, p. 320):

Spelled out again in these letters in rare clarity is that father-son theme which can be found at critical times in the lives of all great innovators as an intrinsic part of their inner transformation.

The value of a case study[1] such as Gandhi's lies in its potential generalization to present a pattern of developmental process which can be used as a model. Gandhi's case affords us an unique opportunity to see the predispositions and special succorance qualities which affected his future greatness and resulted in the highest sense of social obligation in producing Gandhi's "Mahatmaship." The key issue is the presence of the necessary environmental factors required to continue the developmental escalation of such individuals. Fortuitous environmental stimulation at every phase and stage of development may be necessary to bring even the superior and mentally healthy individual to the far heights of full self-actualization of his unique powers. For the rest of us, such lack stunts our final development and limits our creative potential to the workaday world, to a householder's life and to an occasional esthetic experience.

Such a view shows that the study of creativity is conceived as a process which encourages the mental escalation of the adult development of the superior individual. Whereas the average adult ceases this escalation at about the time he ceases physical growth, the creative person retains the ability to reach these higher stages. Perhaps the adolescent developmental phase is extended over that of the average man in a way similar to the extended time of the average human over the average primate. Since the levels reached by extraordinary individuals are not the product of physical development, they are not "natural" in the usual sense. They must be cultivated by happy accidents or by broader opportunities of environmental stimulation, of which civilization itself is a fair example.

One might think of a child's balloon which rather naturally assumes a token shape when a moderate amount of air is introduced, but which can be made to swell up much more by increased pressure. The stages in this paranatural development characterized by complexity of value and transitions from egocentric to altruistic concerns are numerous. They require continuous or recurring crisis situations with strong emotional valence and demand the courage and free energy to face incessant challenge. One is reminded of the long and thorny path to sainthood, and, as is true of so many of the world's great souls, St. Francis, the Cure of Ars, Thoreau, and Gandhi, to mention only a few, that ultimate success is frequently preceded by failure.

We have attempted with only indifferent success in this section to discuss and open an issue obscured by both cultural and personal difficulties. The cultural difficulties are in part due to the fact that the language contains no words properly to express the issue. The personal aspects are clouded by the fact that our culture puts pressure on males to be strong and masculine and any deviation from this norm is suspect and tends to induce guilt in the individual. The issue of foetalization and its differential application to the superior individual is, nevertheless, a very important one; and one may hope that these clumsy initial attempts may later be succeeded by more deft and informed analysis.

---

[1]From pages 102 and 320 of Erikson, E. G., *Gandhi's Truth: On the Origin of Militant Nonviolence*, Copyright, 1969, W. W. Norton Co. Used by permission.

SUMMARY

The "wave of the future" is exemplified by the superior individual in his development. For by his own efforts for more environmental stimulation and the differential "foetalization" assigned to him, he experiences the evolutionary thrust in store for future generations of men. Pointing the march as scout and vanguard is lonely and sometimes dangerous. Throughout the ages, superior individuals confronted with the threat of loneliness and estrangement from their fellows have selected nature, art, meditation and social service as meaningful interests in their development. These roads are not traveled without trial and transformation, without self-doubt and testing. They offer continued escalation and larger satisfactions in life.

In his development, the uncommon man often faces lack of understanding by his fellows. Early efforts to find himself and to integrate his life are apt to be viewed as failures by more philistine age-mates, who accept nothing outside conventional patterns of marriage or business. Artists, poets, philosophers and religious leaders typically face difficulties in vocational crystalization and may spend a large part of their lives in what appears to be an aimless search. They withdraw from society at this time and are often considered failures or outcasts. Thus Jesus spent time in the wilderness; St. Francis had a long illness; the Cure of Ars was a conscientious objector and a fugitive; Whitman an itinerant; Mark Twain a rover; Thoreau a recluse; and hundreds more famous men shared this judgment as youths. Alienation from society, a necessary phase in the withdrawal and return cycle of creativity, produces an acute sense of aloneness in creative people.

Do developmental stages apply to all mankind or only to Western culture? Developmental stage theory applies most completely to those persons and cultures which are most advanced, and least to those least advanced. Those most advanced go more thoroughly through each stage and yet progress through more stages; those least advanced go more superficially through each stage and yet progress through fewer stages. One would not expect a cretin or an Australian bushman to have marked developmental stages in his life. One would expect just the opposite from Gandhi or Lincoln. The crisis at each stage appears more intense for the able person. Many average boys, for example, scarcely show oedipal anxiety during the initiative stage, while gifted boys often evidence a marked crisis followed by oedipal resolution.

This chapter has discussed what man may do for others and for himself by seeking environmental stimulation to maintain his development to self-actualization. It has also discussed what the thrust of evolution has done for the species through the extended process of "foetalization" for superior man. We are concerned here with what man may do, not with what he may fail to do. The onward course of evolutionary progress is signaled by the differential character of developmental tasks performed by outstanding individuals. Was not Jesus himself called an exemplar? That most of us may never reach the final stage of ego-integrity does not mean that self-actualization is unimportant or insignificant for the human race. For it is this lodestone that points the direction of man's progress. As Paul Klee so well says: "I do not wish to represent man as he is, but only as he might be."

6

THE PENALTIES
OF
NONCREATIVITY

To him that hath shall be given, and from him that hath not shall be taken away even that which he hath.

— Jesus

One might think that although creative production may be the highest branch of the development tree, those not acceding to this ultimate might yet find some modicum of satisfaction. Apparently, however, the laws of reality are those discovered many years ago: "To him that hath shall be given, and from him that hath not shall be taken away even that which he hath." In this chapter we shall analyze some of the problems and penalties which beset those who in one way or another fail to actualize the creative gift. These penalties, like the rewards, appear in a graded sequence. To understand them properly we need to examine the individual's use of energy on developmental tasks either at or below his appropriate age.

ENGAGED, DISPLAYED, DEGRADED OR WASTED ENERGY DEFINED

Energy is defined as *engaged* when expended on a developmental task at the stage appropriate for the age level. We say of the person that he is working.

Energy is defined as *displayed* (as a fountain displays) when it is expended on a developmental task one stage below the age. We say of the person that he is playing.

Energy is defined as *degraded* (as a river degrades its banks) when expended on a developmental task characteristic of two stages below age. We say of the individual that he is regressing.

Energy is defined as *wasted* when expended on a developmental task characteristic of a stage earlier than two stages below level. We say of the person that he is arrested.

Thus genital sexual activity is engaged and worked on at the intimacy (sixth) stage, where it is expected; displayed, when continued at the generativity (seventh) stage; and degraded when it persists at the ego-integrity (eighth) stage. The utilization or engagement, as contrasted with the display, degradation or waste of a significant portion of vital energy is a key to undertaking the individual's progress toward self-actualization and creative development. Note the word "significant"; obviously, man is to be judged by his best phase, not his weakest one. All of us must unstring the bow at times. Minor regressions are minor vices, perhaps even useful if they preserve balance in an individual life style.

Some may object that this definition is too harsh and precise; but we feel it is well to be exact in the theoretical formulation and be more tolerant and lenient in our judgment of the human behavior approximating it.

INEFFICIENT DISPLAY OF ENERGY: COMPENSATION

The first, lightest and most common *decalage* is an inefficient use of energy in display on a task one stage below expectation. Frequently this experience is highly pleasant because the individual has learned the "rules of the game" and can play it to perfection. Most sports and hobbies are in this category; indeed most activities on which affluent people spend money constitute display. There is much of the concept of compensation here: "Look, I may not be creative, but see how well I can do this trivial thing."

Display activities, besides being pleasant, are not harmful; they may even serve society, and they have the advantage of play therapy. They protect the noncreative mind from worse feelings and actions by keeping it occupied. While in a sense compensatory, they all involve one unfortunate aspect: they require the individual to assign an inflated importance to the activity to prevent despondency over failure to make life more meaningful, which is to say, more self-actualized. Most of us live our lives in this way—in "quiet desperation" to use Thoreau's term—so occupied with trivial pleasantries which divert the mind that there is no need for us to take the risk of being creative.

BOREDOM AND ENNUI: RATIONALIZATION

If the first stage like limbo is not all that bad, with the second, we start the true descent to Avernus. For here we begin to find the block and blankness which Schneider (1950, p. 126) has so well described as

> . . . the unconscious refusal out of injury, fear or hate to make the specific binding step in the press of the challenging of real and valid (as opposed to neurotic) competition—and inhibiting refusal and a refusing inhibition dedicated to the escape downward into an infantile solution.[1]

The person in this state will tell you that he has no way to turn, that there is nothing for him to do, that he is blocked, facing blank walls with no chance of escape. This is the purest rationalization; but if you attempt to help him, he will attack you because, in helping him to realize that the excuses are specious, you destroy the cocoon of safety wherein he has locked himself from the real world.

Frequently in a situation like this the individual will tell you that he has suffered a power loss, either somatically or psychologically. He is unable to perform in some significant aspect of his life. He becomes hypochondriacal; he seeks refuge in a mild chronic complaint which excuses him from having to face unpleasant reality. His attitude is: "I deserve sympathy and noncombatant status, so give me attention and consideration, and don't expect anything from me, and maybe the developmental tasks of my maturity will go away by themselves."

Many men whose sense of identity is based upon their physical or sexual prowess begin to take on this attitude as they age. It is a more comfortable one than some others such as despair and, while weakening to the individual, it is passive and not socially destructive or addictive in the sense that alcohol or drugs would be. It is, however, the riding of a hobby horse; in the carousel of life we tend to end up riding hobby horses—they go up and down and around and around, but never really get anywhere.

Those who are not productively creative are sometimes very ingenious in their attempts not to be creative, as is brilliantly pointed out by the scientist Henry Eyring (Anderson, 1959, p. 4):

> Only lack of interest or of time or an overwhelming ineptitude deters the prospective investigator from the creative process. Usually the excuses given for failure betray an amazing inventive talent and a vivid imagination. Such brilliant efforts are worthy of better causes.

A youth who has not solved the identity crisis of the fifth period can hardly be expected to make the cognitive escalation from formal operations into the creativity accompanying the sixth stage (intimacy). This is a common complaint of the "square person" or conformist, who is able to fit into a conventional job but who has great difficulty in finding out who he is operationally. Sometimes, happily, in the thirties he works his way out of the identity crisis and escalates into a new kind of power, becoming creative. In other instances, the conflict

---

[1]From page 126, Schneider, Daniel E. *The Psychoanalyst and the Artist*, Copyright, 1950, Farrar, Straus and Giroux. Used by permission.

wages on, taking its toll of mental health until the beginning signs of age and deterioration provoke a real crisis, and he may have a mental or physical break-down or some similar marital or vocational blowup. Because this kind of arrest is more or less sanctioned by our society, the person will feel that he is normal and hence in the right, and he must misinterpret his experience and the motives of others to account for his lot.

IMMATURITY OR SENILITY, ENVY, RESENTMENT OR DESPAIR: PROJECTION

The next step down the scale of wasted powers is that of developing envy, resentment or despair and the onset of other negative emotions which may later rise to destructive levels. Blame for the situation is projected outside the self onto others or the environment, for the individual's intellectual integrity has become distorted. He must misinterpret reality to maintain his "miserable truce" with respect to it. It is not he who is responsible for his problems; it is other people, particularly those with more success or fame. No matter what occurs, it is twisted and distorted because the stereotypes are in, and the script must be made to conform to them.

Extensive projection of blame creates a pronounced shift away from maturity either back to immature behavior or into senility depending on age and, hence, the damage is real and often permanent. The individual's hostility is confined to himself; it is not acted out, but internalized. The illness has set in, but it is quiescent.

A conventional adult, having achieved identity, and able to deal with formal operations, which are both characteristic of the fourth stage, might be thought of as a normal and healthy person, even though he never advanced to creative performance, the intimacy stage or any higher developmental characteristics.

One might think that one could become a conventional adult, having achieved identity and able at least to deal with the formal operations (also characteristic of the fourth stage) and, while not advancing to creative performance, intimacy or any of the higher characteristics, still get by as a normal person. But failure to become creative, like failure to attain intimacy, is to fail and fall short of full development. Those who resist full development and remain at a regressed level are condemned to some of the immature behaviors characteristic of those who have stopped growing and who have started to atrophy.

One aspect of such a person is incipient authoritarianism, which expects simplistic answers to complex questions and which tends to view others as means not ends. These persons find no spontaneity or *joie de vivre* in living, appear boxed into a business or marriage, as contrasted with the creative individual's open ended, dynamic, happy style of life. The penalty for failure to grow and develop is in some sense to be cut off from the stream of life.

RAGE AND DESTRUCTIVENESS:
AUTHORITARIANISM, DISPLACEMENT

Rage and destructiveness, an acting out of an inner authoritarianism as a form of psychological displacement, is a common scene in contemporary American society. Much of the violence found in our culture is due to a perverted creativity expressed through the wrong channels and vented on the wrong objects at the wrong place and time.

The authoritarian formulates idealism or devotion to an in-group leader. The goals of this leader completely overshadow all other imperatives and value systems so that it is proper to kill, bomb, rape, or do anything else to members of the out-group who must first be vilified (such as police). Nothing is done to in-group members even when they break codes of behavior, but anything is possible toward out-groups. An exaggerated concern with destructiveness for its own sake and with weapons which destroy, such as guns or knives, is also evident. Instead of healthy participation in sports, there is an inclination to become spectators at the gorier spectacles, where death or injury may result. There is a fascination with orgies, tortures, deaths, reminiscent of the Nazis. And always there is psychological displacement, the shift of hostility from one object to another which becomes a scapegoat. This indeed is the only explanation for the senseless murders, bombings and other violence perpetrated randomly upon innocent victims.

NEUROSIS OR PSYCHOSIS: FUGUE OR FLIGHT

In the final stage, the problem has become so serious, and the repressed and unconscious burdens so heavy, that the preconscious is in danger of dissolving, leaving the individual in a severe neurotic or psychotic state with reality distortion so severe that he needs professional help. There may be blocking of memory channels and physical or psychological flight with amnesia. Often these symptoms are accompanied by deranged thinking, inappropriate emotional response, ideas of reference and similar symptoms. Creative energy has become completely degraded and internalized so that it is used to heat up the internal environment until the individual cannot stand it any longer. Regression and a complete breakdown of mental health often accompanies the symptoms.

Erikson (Evans, 1966, p. 56) felt that psychic disorder is related to developmental status. Adolescent schizophrenia and adult paranoia, as well as extreme obsessive-compulsive disorders, he viewed as characteristic of arrest at a developmental crisis beyond which "the individual does not seem able to adjust." Erikson believed that a crisis in each stage is necessary before resolution to a higher stage can occur. Believing that the crisis may be a symptom of underlying difficulties such as have just been discussed, this writer is not so sure that the crisis need exist in persons of excellent mental health.

What Erikson may have been referring to, without perhaps having grasped the full significance of his statement, is the *periodicity* of crisis brought about by characteristics shared by developmental periods three stages removed from one another and, hence, in the same columnar family.

Thus autism (developing during the second or autonomy period), dementia praecox (developing during the fifth or identity period), and senile depression (developing during the eighth or ego-integrity period) are three correlated manifestations of an impaired integration of energy into a weakened ego during an identity period crisis. Increased anxiety, as the ego attempts to make sense out of its previous involvement in the world of experience (during the trust, industry and generativity periods respectively), stunts the ability of the ego to develop sufficient power to bring conceptual order and organization to experience.

The resultant state is a schizophrenic-like immobilization, seen alike in the mechanistic behavior of the autistic child and the catatonic seizures of the adolescent schizophrenic in which the individual gives up trying to find his identity as a foil for his environment because he feels himself completely at the mercy of it instead of in control of it. The nightmare quality of the Sullivanian "not me" extends itself even into the *Mitwelt* of the Existentialists—the world of interrelationships and communication—frightening and traumatizing the individual and forcing him to withdraw still farther and seek a new environment within his body, or in an artificial language or in mechanistic movements and relations. The opposite of the creative individual, he is completely immobilized.

An excellent summary of the individual in this stage has been made by Sadler (1969, p. 68):

> In contrast to the openness of focal attention in play there are various forms of ordinary perception which have become hardened through habit, cultural pressures, and the dread of anxiety. Psychoanalytic studies in particular have illuminated the grave threats to truly creative perception and existence. When we experience anxiety, particularly in massive doses, considerable distortion occurs which closes our eyes to certain areas of our personal world. Defense mechanisms are brought into operation which project unrelated meanings upon an immediate situation, leading the anxious person unconsciously to interpret his experience arbitrarily. When anxiety strikes, rather than develop focal attention, we are prone to engage in what Harry Stack Sullivan called "selective inattention." By being selectively inattentive we refuse to perceive what is really given, and thus fail to profit from experience.[1]

PSYCHOPATHOLOGY AND REMISSION: SELF-RENEWAL

If the foregoing has seemed despondent, let us continue with a note of hope. There are penalties for noncreative and nonactualized performance in the world of reality but, like other penalties, they can be remitted by good works. If there is psychopathology in the world, there is also remission of sin and symptom, and the process of self-renewal is held out to all who want to try again.

It is not so much that creative people are free from psychopathology, anxiety and stress as that they have devised some way to live with it. As Barron

---

[1]From page 68, Sadler, W. A., "Creative Existence: Play as a Pathway to Personal Freedom," Copyright *Humanitas* 5:57–80, 1969. Used by permission.

(1968) says:

> This concept of balancing anxiety with creativity instead of letting one destroy or cancel the other is much like the modern man's finances—he has both liabilities and assets and has learned to live; he doesn't just cash in his chips. After all, we only have to pay the interest on our debts at any one time, and it is this forward thrusting of psychological commutation (sometimes at high interest rates) that distinguishes the creative person from the merely anxious (or is it just the courage to try?).

At any rate, the process of self-renewal is available to anyone at any time, starting from the corner where you are. It may not make you highly creative, for that option may be past, but it will certainly help you to better mental health, which is the first prerequisite of creativity.

Virtue can be made of nothing more than necessity. Every egregious style is the result of remediated defect. This principle of psychology is as true in the improvement of lives as it is in the improvement of baseball batting. Knowing one's weakness is the first step to overcoming it. We surmount it by analyzing its components and then rearranging them into a new order to work for us, not against us. Hence we transform the situation into a problem capable of solution, not a crisis requiring a miracle.

A refrigerator operates like a heat pump which separates hot and cold air. The hot air is dissipated harmlessly into the room, while the cold air makes the refrigerator operate properly. The creativity cycle runs in a similar way with the positive aspect focused and the negative aspect dissipated. There are people who would like to be creative who do just the opposite—they dissipate their positive forces and focus their negative ones, thus becoming negative, wasteful and destructive. The solution is not to shoot them and start again but to help them learn to reverse the cycle. The problem in setting ourselves free to become creative (and later self-actualized) is not to destroy our encultured behavior matrix but to assign it to a higher value and service. Self-actualization is a more positive thing than the mere suppression of all negative idiosyncrasies.

Someone once humorously remarked that the reason we have to work with people is that there are not enough angels to go around. Individuals who come into the process of self-actualization are not necessarily perfect; like nine-day kittens their eyes have been opened, but their faces are frequently dirty. Self-actualization involves a major positive stance toward the process of becoming, but, while that tends to cut off the power for idiosyncratic reaction and cultural stereotypes, it does not apply the brakes to a wheel already heavy with rotational inertia. Sometimes these holdovers are enough to keep the individual permanently in the vestibule of self-actualization, sometimes they are merely mild enough to act like esters in whisky and impart an idiosyncratic flavor or bouquet, and sometimes they are fragrant enough merely to suggest the human origin of the saint. But as most persons who come into the process of self-actualization are not perfect, we need to look at some of the outcomes of the less than perfect state in these people.

The ability to cope with stress and to surmount anxiety must be regarded as an aspect of positive mental health which leads toward self-actualization. It is often enhanced rather than diminished by adversity, for if the greater challenge can be met, the response must be greater also. In this process the person discovers a deeper self, with new perceptions and new relationships to outer events that enables him to transcend the crisis with enhanced power and, hence, an increased self-confidence.[1]

Viewed from another angle, the renewal process enables human beings to demonstrate their ego-strength and creativity. Like a spinning gyroscope which resists deflection from its axis of rotation and quickly restores itself when interfered with, this ability of renewal is a sign of health and developmental potentiality on the pathway toward fulfillment. It is a remarkable and hopeful sign how often human beings, though taxed severely in a crisis situation, are able to muster emergency powers and rally their forces to make a supreme response and recover their mental health and self-esteem. There is something of great dignity and value in this process, something to make us all realize that, though man may make mistakes and fall, he can, in this open-ended universe, also rise again—something to give us hope in place of despair and courage in place of fear. It suggests that the rational view of the universe is optimistic not pessimistic, that man may always live by taking the offensive against his environment, and that life is not an idyll of the flesh but an adventure of the spirit.

DEVELOPMENTAL PROCESS AND ARREST[2]

Those of us who deal with young people and their problems can best discharge our responsibilities by attempting better to understand developmental process and its implications for the guidance of all children and then modify our treatment or therapy in terms of the individual differences we find upon diagnosis of a particular child. Guidance problems, not the result of cultural aspects, do not occur by chance but are the products of discontinuities in the child's development. What we are attempting here, therefore, is a synoptic view of such problems which relates them to developmental theory in a systematic manner.

Let us review some key concepts of development. Development differs from growth in involving a change in quality, whereas growth involves a change of quantity. The apple ripens as well as enlarges. The concept of development involves escalation over time. The new stage is not merely progression but also the unfoldment of new ideas and motifs. Development may be considered as a quantum effect with identifiable levels and states instead of a smooth curve of accretion. Moreover, each stage contains characteristics appropriate for its full efflorescence and embraces the germinal material for the development of the next stage. Thus each stage is the necessary, but not the sufficient, precursor of the next.

---

[1] This paragraph is credited to Sybil Richardson.

[2] This section has been revised and expanded from an article "The Guidance of Creative Children," originally appearing in *The Journal of the Association of Women Deans and Counselors*, 31:154–61, Summer 1968. Used by permission.

The environment is the sufficient cause: its resources, the opportunities and dangers it offers determine if, when and to what extent the next stage will evolve. Let us imagine a healthy child at any particular developmental stage. At this time, he may be affected by the environment as follows:

(1)   Lethally, that is, he may be killed;

(2)   Stunted, that is, his further physical, emotional or intellectual development may be stopped so that he remains permanently at the present stage;

(3)   Blighted, that is, while there may be further development, there will not be further escalation; the developmental sequence has been damaged;

(4)   Partially successful, that is, the child will go on, but with developmental arrest, such as trauma, distortions, stigmata, neurotic tendencies or behaviors;

(5)   Successful, but only after strong effort and emotional expenditure, in which case the child's interests and attitudes will be haunted by an affective "ghost" organized around the continued emotional aura required to complete the task. The adult "anal" personality is an example, as is the interest formulation postulated by Roe in her theory of vocational choice;

(6)   Fully successful without difficulty;

(7)   Overly successful, that is the child may come to enjoy so much the tasks and successes of this period that they and not the onward course of development become the goal for him. This condition makes it difficult for him to incorporate and integrate the lessons of this stage into the succeeding ones. The failure is not at this stage but one of integrating the stage into the ongoing developmental process. Many children will be completely successful at a stage without having it in any way interfere with their ongoing progress. While we do not speculate on the causes of the lack of integration here, it does not appear to be due to a complete immersion in the tasks of the stage or in their success, but rather, perhaps to overprotectiveness or a binding type of love or transference which becomes attached to a stage process or task.

If Erikson's developmental stage theory truly reflects the course of personality maturation from infant trust to senior integrity, it suggests the focus of counseling in terms of individuals who evidence a graduated series of developmental arrests. Each arrested stage presumably has its own psychological and social characteristics and, hence, its own diagnosis and therapy.

The social penalties for arrested development decrease in magnitude at higher levels. At later stages, when more complex developments are arrested, the effects are less crucial to the individual's basic functioning and, hence, less serious. Such a taxonomy of developmental psychopathology could result in clear diagnosis of causes and subsequent formulation of specific treatment modes. Finally, such a system would have much to say about the most desirable "press" of an institution on development. Are the objectives of the school (as felt by the child, not as listed in the catalog) at harmony with the child's development, or are they at cross-purposes to it and, therefore, often a hindrance?

In building such a scheme, let us start with Erikson's eight stages (figure 9), remembering Anne Roe's words (1957) that the origin of interests "depends on the way psychic energies come involuntarily to be expended." It is the twist that is given to psychic energy as the individual passes through each of the stages which produces idiosyncratic development and possible arrest. Relative success at each stage incorporates a new strength into the ego, while relative failure at any stage leaves part of the ego there, and the rest carries on with a certain diminished weakness, as failure at socialization during the industry period might leave one unsure of oneself in public when an adult.

Ideally, each person would progress through life as one does through a croquet game, passing successive wickets, and finally arriving at the finish peg. Most of us, however, get stopped somewhere in the croquet game of life. We either fail repeatedly to negotiate a wicket, or we become diverted there and use our turn to "play rover" (hit the balls of other players). There are thus two kinds of failure at developmental tasks: simple failure differentiation of task (missing a wicket) and failure to integrate an overly successful stage into succeeding ones (playing rover). It is as if the child learns the skills and games of a particular stage so well that they and not the process of development become reality for him, and he wants to keep playing them, for their own sake, after the time for playing them is over. The poet, Longfellow, described the situation in *Nature*:

> *As a fond mother when the day is o'er*
> *Leads by the hand her little child to bed,*
> *Half willing, half reluctant to be led*
> *And leave his broken playthings on the floor*
> *Still gazing at them through the open door*
> *Not wholly reassured or comforted*
> *By promises of others in their stead*
> *Which though more splendid may not please him more,*
> *So nature deals with us and takes away*
> *Our playthings one by one . . . .*

The diagram related Eriksonian concepts to developmental arrests distinguishing two kinds of failure—failure at differentiation (the first type) and failure at integration (the last type). (It would have been possible to have constructed a more elaborate chart with each of the seven kinds of developmental outcomes sketched, instead of the polar two at the continuum ends.) The first column represents approximate ages; second comes the Eriksonian stage; third is the typology caused by failure to differentiate (achieve the task); fourth is the typology caused by failure to integrate the task (move to the next stage). Finally the governing morality is indicated. This may be defined as the ethos value or emotional complex which has contributed to the individual's failure at the task or makes him unable to go on to the next stage. Each of these developmental arrests gives rise to a particular type of counseling case, so that we come, perhaps for the first time, to be able to organize counseling cases into a developmental hierarchy.

Approximate Age	Stage	Failure at Differentiation	Failure at Integration of a Success into Next Stage	Morality
0–2	Trust	Schizoid person	Overdependent neurotic	Fear
2–4	Autonomy	Neurotic doubt of self worth	Anal person	Shame
4–7	Initiative	Guilt immobilized person	Creative nonconformist	Guilt
7–M	Industry	Underachiever	Overachiever—grind type	Puritan ethic
Teens	Identity	Alienated introvert	Moody, "Permanent adolescent" "Social butterfly"	Socialization
20s	Intimacy	Don Juan man Frigid woman	Nonpaternal man Nonmaternal woman	Sexual love
30s	Generativity (parental)	Parent who competes with child	The child-oriented woman of fifty	Children
40s	Ego integrity	The senior depressive	(Modern "saints" such as Eleanor Roosevelt or Dr. Schweitzer)	Altruism

[a] Ideally each person should go through life as in a croquet game, passing each wicket. One can fail to negotiate wickets (failure at differentiation) and also stop and play rover (failure at integration). The latter person has been so successful at a particular stage that he keeps at it instead of incorporating it into the next stage of on-going development.

Figure 9. Eriksonian Stages and Their Counseling Problems[a]

Figure 9 depicts a hierarchy in which failures at the first two stages produce psychotics and neurotics; at the next two stages, give rise to problems in school guidance; and in the third two, cause difficulties in university and adult life. The sequence suggests that the "press" of most institutions of higher learning should be stress on socialization and not merely intellectualization. Finally, the table infers that some problems are not developmental but cultural, among these aggression, delinquency, drugs and dropouts. The counselor, as developmental specialist, may here gain some argument for suggesting that these problems are not primarily his to deal with except in collaboration with other social and cultural agencies.

Problems of development (which are the true guidance problems) arise from obstructions, distortions or arrest in the dynamics of development itself. Such behaviors as aggression, which may be socially disapproved by the majority culture and, hence, a problem to it, often represent the healthy struggle by the individual for such development as he can make in his milieu. Aggressiveness is likely to be a pseudo-problem reflecting a societal judgment than a true distortion of development.[1]

Since the writer is more interested in illustrating the relationship between developmental stage theory and guidance than in pursuing the model further, readers are invited to explore other applications of the theory to the practice of pupil personnel services. This action will assist in displaying the relationship between developmental theory in general and individual counseling cases in particular. But because these developmental models refer to the onward progress of youth and young adults, marriage counselors and vocational rehabilitation workers (as well as other mental health ministries dealing with the full functioning of adults) will find use in the effective application of developmental theory to their clients. From this may be expected to develop a new "metaguidance," concerned not merely with school personnel services but with the whole development of individuals, and not just with the eradication of psychopathology but with the development of fully functioning, self-actualized people.

SUMMARY

No one who looks thoughtfully at the present scene can doubt that something like growing pains is occurring to the whole psychotherapy-guidance-mental health movement. Whether one looks at the "hippies" or the vogue of ecology or existentialism, or the Esalen-type workshops, or basic encounter groups, or other similar movements, there is a new push in the area of adult humanistic development—something distinct from the mere eradication of psychopathology— a new cult, of which Maslow is the prophet.

The concepts of the mental health ministries have heretofore centered in the removal of abnormal aspects of adulthood or in the solving of developmental

---

[1] This paragraph is credited to Sybil Richardson.

crisis problems. But this view is too narrow for the metaguidance required for self-actualization. The old bears the same relationship to the new that muscular therapy for the physically handicapped does to physical culture for the strong and aspiring athlete. There is need of a new term (here called metaguidance), not to solve crisis situations but to aid in the developmental process for full adulthood. This concept has been glimpsed in such phrases as "developmental guidance," "humanistic education," "encounter therapy," "reevaluation therapy," "maintenance guidance," and "co-counseling." It involves healthy people using mental health services to make themselves even healthier and more creative, thus assuring escalation into the self-actualized later stages. As an athlete needs training to maintain and develop skills of strength, so this metaguidance provides the stimulation to insure that mental and moral development will not cease when physical development is over.

In this chapter we have explored the problems and penalties which accrue from lack of creativity, which is to say, lack of development into the full powers and freedom of adulthood. We have seen that these range in a series of graded steps from the seriousness of complete immobilization and psychosis to the lotus-land happiness of the merely uncreative. We have presented a categorization of guidance problems in terms of developmental arrest, involving both failure to differentiate and failure to integrate the characteristic tasks of a given stage. Finally, we have pointed to the fact that, whereas guidance of the past as well as all of psychotherapy, has been mainly concerned with the eradication of psychopathology, the mental health ministry of the future will be more concerned with developing the full potential of the individual to the self-actualization of the last three adult developmental stages. Despite the negative tone of this chapter, it is important to end on this positive note—one in which health is not merely regarded as the absence of sickness but a positive necessity for man's fullest development. A final chapter has been reserved for the exploration of that self-actualized process.

7

THE MANSION
OF SELF-
ACTUALIZATION

Build thee more stately mansions, Oh my soul
As the swift seasons roll;
Leave thy low-vaulted past;
Let each new temple, nobler than the last
Shut thee from heaven with a dome more vast,
Till thou at length art free,
Leaving thine outworn shell by life's unresting sea.

— Oliver Wendell Holmes

SELF-ACTUALIZATION DEFINED AS PERTAINING
TO THE LAST THREE STAGES

Self-actualization was defined by Maslow as the act of manifesting the capabilities for which one had the potentiality. The structure of our language predisposes us to think in terms of those who finally reach self-actualization, as contrasted with those who merely get to the vestibule of the mansion and wait. But like other more mathematical limits, self-actualization is better measured by the differential than the functional. Hence, a better way of conceptualization is to look at the process, not the end product, and to distinguish those in whom the process is wholly developed as self-actualized.

In discussion of the sixth (creative), seventh (psychedelic) and eighth (illuminative) cognitive stages, we are on new and insufficiently explored ground; hence, the reader must be prepared for some confusion in terms. Here the phrase "self-actualization" will be used indiscriminately to refer to operations at all three levels. Actually, the upper reach of the continuum from the stage of creativity onward is open ended, for once an individual reaches the creative stage cognitively, his conscious mind is opened and enlarged, and he gains new horizons and options. The theory of stages becomes much less significant than the study of the process, and for all we know, looking at the system as it were from below, there may be advanced stages or processes that we cannot yet conceive.

We have tried to make tentative identification of the three advanced stages—the sixth or creative, the seventh or psychedelic and the eighth or illuminative. The creative stage has been well described in the literature and is treated at length in chapters 1 and 4. The psychedelic is just now being described in the literature of psychology (Tart, 1969), though it has long been known in the literature of mysticism. The eighth stage is still pretty much unknown territory. Although we can say little about the cognitive processes of the final stage, those processes which are occasional and transitory in the psychedelic period become habitual and fixed in the eighth stage, and thus the doors or barriers between the conscious and preconscious are done away with almost entirely. This stage or process may be referred to as "integral," since the person is truly "whole" or "holy."

Before passing to a detailed analysis of the psychedelic stage, we need to clarify the significance of the unusual. Self-actualization is an unusual process which happens to a few human beings at certain times in their lives. Processes which do not occur to many people, but only to a few, are often considered pathological because they are not "normal." Their rarity may allow them to be considered trivial. Yet giving birth is such a process, occurring to only half or less of the population, and then only at widely spaced times; yet it is perfectly normal, and while unusual is so important as to be vital. The unusual, then, may have extremely important consequences; and self-actualization is an example.

Surprising as it may seem, even the practice of creativity may have a stultifying effect on development and hence on self-actualization if it involves stagnation in the sixth developmental period instead of the face-to-face encounter with the "not me" required from most of us as a kind of initiation into the psychedelic aspects of the seventh period. Just as many an intellectual, too successful in formal operations to the detriment of his creative or divergent thinking, is content to "shoot fish in a barrel," so a considerable number of creative people seem content to dwell in that stage, occupied with the rationality of problem-solving, and the many outlets and activities which creative production affords for avoiding confrontations with one's preconscious. This portal to psychedelia is too frightening, too alienated from a still somewhat shaky sense of identity to risk such encounter. Such an individual, often the epitome of the Puritan Ethic, will be a real achiever who will dread "to lose control of himself" and who may foreclose psychedelic adventures and development because of this fear. It is hard indeed for humans to learn that each developmental gift is a loan, not a possession, that it is to be savored and sampled, and then traded in on the corresponding gift of the next stage. But a long time ago, somebody with insight about such matters told us plainly: "He that shall seek to save his life, shall lose it."

THE PSYCHEDELIC EXPERIENCE

The psychedelic explanation of creativity is not just another way of looking at the subject; for some people it is *the* way. The mind-expanding aspect is seen as a fundamental property of life, with creativity the aurora of the new day. Barron (1968, p. 305) echoes this view:

> The tendency of life then is toward the expansion of consciousness. In a sense, a description of means for the expansion of consciousness has been the central theme of this book, and it is in this evolutionary tendency that such diverse phenomena as psychotherapy, surprising or unexpected self-renewal, the personally evolved and deepened forms of religious belief, creative imagination, mysticism, and deliberately induced changes of consciousness through the use of chemicals find a common bond.[1]

Barron sees creativity as one of the psychedelic aspects of the person. He is perhaps at his best in his research into originality (1968, chapters 16 and 17). He hypothesizes that persons characterized as originals have a greater preference for complexity, are more complex as persons, have independence of judgment, are self-assertive and dominant, and reject suppression to control impulse. He concludes (1968, p. 224):

> Thus the creative genius may be at once more naive and knowledgeable, being at home equally to primitive symbolism and to rigorous logic. He is both more primitive and more cultured, more destructive and more constructive, occasionally crazier, and yet adamantly saner than the average person.[2]

Long ago Emerson described this when he remarked in "The Poet" (1950, p. 330):

> It is a secret that every intellectual man quickly learns that beyond the energy of his possessed and conscious intellect, he is capable of a new energy (as by an intellect doubled upon itself) by abandonment to the nature of things; that beside his privacy of power as an individual man, there is a greater public power on which he can draw, by unlocking, at all risks, his human doors, and suffering the ethereal tides to roll and circulate through him. . . . For if in any manner we can stimulate this . . . new passages are opened for us into nature; the mind flows into and through things hardest and highest and the metamorphosis is possible.

---

[1]From page 305 of Barron, F. *Creativity and Personal Freedom*, Copyright 1968, Litton Educational Publishing Co. Used by permission.

[2]*Ibid.*, p. 224.

> This is the reason why bards love wine, mead, narcotics, coffee, tea, opium and the fumes of sandalwood and tobacco, or whatever other procurers of animal exhilaration. All men avail themselves of such means as they can to add this extraordinary power to their normal powers; and to this end they prize conversation, music, pictures, sculpture, dancing, theatre, travelling, war, mobs, fires, gaming, several coarser or finer quasi-mechanical substitutes for the true nectar, which is the ravishment of the intellect. . . .

Three terms are in use to describe these experiences: (1) psychedelic or mind-expanding (which is preferred, because it clearly suggests the altered and enlarged dimensions made available to the conscious mind when the doors to the preconscious swing open); (2) illumination (used by Bucke for much the same experience, but one better reserved for the steady state of the eighth stage); and (3) peak experience (used by Maslow to indicate a special kind of affective experience with unusual, vivid, or highly significant import).

Maslow (Mooney and Razik, 1967, p. 49 ff) describes some of the characteristics of persons having peak experiences. He lists them as "giving up the past, giving up the future, innocence, a narrowing of consciousness, loss of self-consciousness, disappearance of fear, lessening of defenses, strength and courage, acceptance thrust, receptivity, integration, ability to dip into the preconscious, aesthetic perceiving, spontaneity, expressiveness, and fusion with the world."

Foster (1968, p. 116) after a survey of the relationships of creative persons concluded: "Self-actualization, like true psychological health, requires both creativity and human relatedness."

Panhke and Richards (Tart, 1969, p. 406) point out nine qualities of the genuine mystic experience as: (1) unity, (2) objectivity, (3) spatial and temporal transcendence, (4) sacredness, (5) positive mood valence, (6) paradoxicality, (7) ineffability, (8) transiency, and (9) positive later changes in behavior. "One's faith in one's potential for creative achievement tends to be increased."

Mogar (Tart, 1969, p. 397) cites some research on the area.

> With regard to positive revelatory experiences, Maslow recently developed the thesis that experiences referred to as religious, mystical or transcendental actually denote special cases of the more generic "core-religious" of peak experiences, described as the hallmark of self-actualized people (Maslow, 1964). Similarly, the extensive research done on creativity by MacKinnon and his associates indicates that the truly creative person is distinguished from the noncreative individual by his capacity for "transliminal experience" (MacKinnon, 1964). Following Harold Rugg's study of creative imagination the transliminal experience is characterized by an illuminating flash of insight occurring at a critical threshold of the conscious-unconscious continuum. MacKinnon's description of the transliminal experience bears a striking resemblance to the more inclusive peak experience. Interestingly, Maslow (1964) suggests that psychedelic drugs may offer means of producing a controlled peak experience under observation, especially in "non-peakers."[1]

---

[1]From page 397, R. E. Mogar, "Current and Future Trends in Psychedelic Research," in C. T. Tart (ed.), *Altered States of Consciousness.* Copyright 1969, John Wiley & Sons. Used by permission.

Maslow himself (Anderson, 1958, p. 90) has this to say:

> Since almost everyone I questioned could remember such an experience (peak), I had to come to the tentative conclusion that many, perhaps most people are capable of temporary states of integration, even of self-actualization, and therefore of self-actualizing creativeness.[1]

Maslow (Mooney and Razik, 1967, p. 53) also remarks:

> Part of the process of integration of the person is the recovery of the unconscious and the preconscious, particularly of the primary process (or poetic, metaphysic, mystic, primitive, archaic, childlike). Our conscious intellect is too exclusively analytic, rational, numerical, atomic, conceptual, and so it misses a good deal of reality especially within ourselves.[2]

Again in describing peak experience Maslow (Mooney and Razik, 1967, p. 47) says:

> It has always been described as a loss of self or ego or sometimes as a transcendence of self. There is fusion with the reality being observed, a oneness, where there was twoness, an integration of some sort with the non-self. There is universally reported a seeing of formerly hidden truths, a revelation in the strict sense, a slipping away of veils, and finally almost always the whole experience is experienced as bliss, ecstasy, rapture or exaltation.[3]

Bucke (1929) was the first to give a semipsychological explanation of some aspects of self-actualization with developmental overtones, although his book *Cosmic Consciousness* was heavily loaded with religious usage. While many of Bucke's ideas are ingenuous or outmoded, the volume deserves consideration because it was one of the first to investigate the topic; hence, a brief review of his ideas is in order.

Bucke felt that the development of superior individuals retraced the development of the race. He believed that as the race was in process of being given the gift of illumination, this phenomenon was now appearing in a few of the most superior individuals at the time of their greatest maturity and mental health. He defined illumination as a mystical conversion-hysteria type of experience, such as occurred to St. Paul on the road to Damascus, and saw it as of a profound religious nature, which afterward produced changes in the individual's life style. He professed to find more incidents of illumination now than in ancient times and concluded (rather ingenuously) that this indicated the race was in the process of receiving this ability. Most of the book consists of case histories of about 45 people, more than half drawn from history and the others known by personal acquaintance. (A similar method was later used by Maslow in his study of self-actualizing people.) Such incidents are more likely to be found in contemporaries; thus only major historical figures from earlier times have any

---

[1]From page 90, A. Maslow, "Creativity in Self-Actualizing People," in H. A. Anderson (ed.), *Creativity and Its Cultivation*. Copyright 1959, Harper & Row Publishers. Used by permission.

[2]A. Maslow, "The Creative Attitude," used by permission of *The Structurist* (Saskatoon: University of Saskatchewan) 3:4–10, 1963.

[3]*Ibid.*

chance of standing as examples.

Aside from the religious explanation, Bucke's book can be criticized psychologically on the ground that he did not realize that somatotypes apparently influence the kind of person who has the more dramatic illuminatory experiences. Thus Bucke leaves Emerson at the "twilight" level because this conversion hysteria was absent, while including others because it was present.

It seems to us that the conversion-hysteria phenomenon, complete with fire and all, may be inevitable for some personalities but unnecessary in others. Some natures require it because of rigid repression in the light of some religious or social code. Doubts or conflicting evidence inconsistent with that code are not forgotten or ignored but are stored in the preconscious. If enough of these pile up, the bonds of repression burst, and conversion to a fully developed code of more freedom and opposite to the previous restrictions seems suddenly to emerge. When the repressive forces are not so strong and clearly organized, the conversion phenomena need not occur.

The essential component of the psychedelic stage or process is a sudden opening of the mind to enlargement, to a grander vista than ever seen before, with a power surge which is analogous to shifting into overdrive in an auto. There has been an acceleration of process, and this acceleration becomes capable of occasional return under proper conditions of environmental stimulation. The interior conditions for this process are that the boundaries between the ego and the preconscious open up and the psychedelic mind expansion is felt because the conscious mind is suddenly master in an enlarged domain.

Despite its methodological limitations, Bucke's book made an early contribution which focused on development, on high mental health, on superior individuals and on rare talents. He realized that because an experience is rare, it is not unreal, but only unusual, and hence an excellent guidepost to new and uncharted developments. This is a scientific principle of the first magnitude, as useful in the behavioral as the natural sciences. (One has only to recall helium, radium and U-238 for illustrative purposes.)

Bucke often talked of superior individuals who lived in the "twilight" of illumination but on whom the full sun of enlightenment had never risen. This judgment was made because they never reported an ecstatic experience. Now we know that certain psychological types are more prone to these experiences than others, as Maslow (1967) reported. While experiences are often found in those in the process of self-actualization, nevertheless it seems also true that some in the process do not have them at all.

Evidently the process of self-actualization covers a wide track, broad enough for many different kinds of people. For one it will mean a continuous cycle of occasional creative flashes followed by longer rests; for another, genuine psychedelic or peak experiences accompanied by increases in power, energy and creativity; for a third it may mean an opening between the conscious and preconscious which either becomes systematic or habitual under certain stimuli or is amenable to control from the conscious side. None of these is to be preferred above the others, for all who dwell within the vestibule of the mansion are blessed. Those who come to self-actualization late in life, say, after 45, may never have the ecstasy appropriate for the generativist period, but live happy, constructive and productive lives nevertheless.

One aspect of the peak experience, whether mystic or otherwise, is that something happens to the ego. Some types of such experience enable the ego to merge with the experience; in others it becomes altered or changed. But however this may be reported, the psychologist realizes that there is communication difficulty because of the uniqueness of the experience, and he suspects that the dimensions of the narrator's own ego have been drastically altered. This inner change throws off his sense of reality orientation because he is, for the time, measuring experience with an expanded yardstick.

Indeed the peak experience is much like the Pentacostal experience and the group encounter experience, all of which depend on a syndrome which:

(1)   brings together a group of lovers, athletes, noviates, etc.;

(2)   develops a high degree of group cohesiveness or esprit —

    (a)   resulting in a breakdown of barriers normally separating people so that

    (b)   there is fluidity and flow and relaxation of ego controls resulting in

    (c)   ecstasy much like a sexual climax

    (d)   followed by relief, quiescence and satiation and

    (e)   an invasion of energy, power or morale which

    (f)   results in a feeling of inner transformation and

    (g)   a changed behavior pattern with superior performance.

Another tendency in those approaching self-actualization often obscures progress. Commonly seen in artists and poets, the creative outpouring of the mind is often extensive during the intimacy period, giving considerable promise of continued rise into higher stages. Then success overtakes the man (more rarely adversity), either of which can stunt further development and deflect the artist from the kind of self-discipline required to activate self-actualization. Sometimes the powers of creativity are so enchanting to the individual that he prefers to toy with them rather than to integrate them into the next advance. Sometimes a too rigorous moral code, a too conventional wife or a too narrow religion keeps the man from the necessary bursting of his cultural bonds. Some famous men have exhibited these tendencies. Wordsworth is a nearly classic example of a poet with remarkable promise when young, whose fame made him conservative and extinguished his powers in the end. Coleridge ruined his artistic ability through drugs and O'Neill through alcohol. Mark Twain was another creative genius who was tortured by the restrictions of a conventional life and cultural mores. Many other examples could be adduced. Too much early success (as noted in a previous chapter) at a particular stage may very easily prevent the individual from leaving the stage easily. This is particularly true of the higher stages because there is often the cultural pressure to accede to them. One tends to want to stay where one's friends are.

Adversity is bad enough for a person, but success is almost always fatal. Fatal to further development, that is, for nothing is more tempting to holding an individual in a given stage than public success or acclaim as a result of exhibiting the characteristic properties of that stage. (This is one reason why narcissistic actresses commit suicide with such frequency as their looks begin to fade.) At least in the lower stages, biological growth tends to accelerate us out of them. But in the higher areas, a man who has become markedly successful at any cognitive level from formal operations onwards may be very reluctant to escalate from that level. There seems to be no reason for him to do so. Life affords him many opportunities to shoot fish in a barrel with skills already honed and perfected. So it is often those who have not been overly successful at the fifth stage who are most ready to make advances which bring success at later stages. It is seldom the successful businessman who becomes the mystic.

This view suggests that there must be a combination of environmental stimulation and individual initiative which never allows a developing individual to relax or stagnate in any given stage. Erikson's study of Gandhi (1969) indicates how the Ahmedabad mill strike performed this service for the budding saint who had the courage to accept the challenge when it was offered. Similar challenges from the environment, and responses from the individual, are present in other historical examples of self-actualization.

ILLUMINATION

To talk about the eighth cognitive stage is a little like a small boy in the initiative period discussing the sexual problems involved in maturation and adolescence. Whatever he may have found out about them through whatever means, it is certain that he will lack the developmental status to make adequate evaluation and draw proper conclusions. Any pronouncements that a psychologist may make about this ultimate stage are as likely to be fraught with misconception like "Looking through a glass darkly." We may, however, draw on a few extrapolations for guidance.

In the first place, we feel that there is a tendency for most writers (and here we include Maslow, Bucke and others) to mistake "illumination" with the psychedelic stage. The dramatic openings of psychedelia are enough to awe anyone. When the mind suddenly finds itself master in an enlarged domain, it may easily suffer "delusions of grandeur." But majestic though this experience must be, it is not illumination. By whatever name the eighth stage is called, its primary characteristic must be that those processes which are spasmodic, occasional and irruptive in the seventh stage must become steady, constant and habitual in the eighth. Illumination means a steady light, not the flickering of a candle or the blinding of the off-again, on-again lighthouse beam. For those of us in lower stages, one can compare the difference between the psychedelic and illuminative states to be somewhat like the difference between the ups and downs of romance, the presence and absence of the beloved before marriage with the steady satisfaction, companionship and contentment of the state of married love.

It is perhaps a mistake even to regard illumination as a stage. Mendeleev, in an early work on his periodic table of the chemical elements, left the table open ended. He could not foresee that the very heavy elements were mostly radioactive and generally disintegrated into other elements lower on the table. Process is certainly likely to be more important than state in this ultimate stage. While ideally the state is a steady one, in practice it is approached by developing individuals in whom the spasmodic and occasional enlightenment of the psychedelic stage tends to become more habitual, although perhaps not completely so.

We gain a bit from the koans of Zen Buddhism here—those mystic sayings and questions which seem to have no logical answer but whose interpretation requires a higher understanding. The Irishman who said: "If you don't go to other people's funerals, they won't come to yours" uttered a statement literally illogical but full of truth on a higher plane. In the illuminative stage, there is likely to be a taking over of the psyche by the preconscious which deemphasizes the rational processes of the conscious mind in favor of intuition, precognitions and an enlarged understanding of the Zen koan type, which throws a diffused floodlight on the world of experience rather than the concentrated spotlight of the rational mind.

There is also a change in ego structure in which the ego loses some of its "I-ness' and becomes, in Roger's phrase, more "The subjective awareness of experience"—in which there is less of the Hobbes "loose and separate" aspect and more unity and connection with all mankind and nature. There is (because of the periodic position of this stage in the identity column) a new identity crisis which arises, but now it is released from its corporate bonding (which is its chrysalis) and is free to become one with others and with the world. Having become sure of who I am, I am now free to merge myself in love and freedom with others and all of life.

TECHNIQUES FOR FACILITATING SELF-ACTUALIZATION

The "American question," as Piaget called it, of whether a good thing can be speeded up developmentally is certainly appropriate. The psychedelic experience seems most likely to occur to young adults in good mental health between the ages of 30 and 40 (Bucke, 1929, p. 81), although it may, of course, occur later. Can we hasten or help this process in ourselves or others? The verdict of history is that we can, and many religious and philosophical systems have been built on the relevant techniques.

These techniques may be divided into three categories: (1) psychomotor, (2) affective and (3) cognitive (which conform to the three areas of the taxonomy of educational objectives) (Bloom, 1956). The opening of research into these categories represents one of the real "fronts" of humanistic psychology.

Psychomotor and Physiological Means

(1)   Drugs, especially LSD, marijuana and peyote. For adequate discussion of these, see Masters and Huston (1966) and Tart (1969). For research on

enhancement of creativity through psychedelic experience see Tart (1969, p. 460 ff), also Krippner (1968) and Otto and Mann (1969, pp. 199–202). (It is important to remember that the word "psychedelic" refers to mind expansion and includes, but is not limited to, the use of drugs.)

(2)   Breathing of carbon dioxide, nitrous oxide or other prepared gas mixtures to produce mild anoxia. (This was the classic method of William James) (1958). See also Barron (1968), p. 148).

(3)   Exposure of eyes to a stroboscopic lamp giving flicker fusion which interferes with EEG waves and produces the state in some (Barron, 1969, p. 148).

(4)   Conscious control of automatic functions such as breathing and heart rate. This is reported in some literature and a focus for future investigation.

Religious, Mystic and Hypnotic Experience

(1)   Religious exercises, especially prayer, fasting, meditation, with possible mortification. Reported in the mystic literature of all religions, especially Hinduism, Christianity and Zen Buddhism.

(2)   Joe Kamiya's conditioning technique of the EEG alpha rhythm control through turning on a light bulb by meditation. This is a major psychological breakthrough since it condenses a long Zen technique of learning to meditate on nothing with only six weeks training; see Tart (1969, p. 507); see also Brown (1970) for further information on this subject.

(3)   Hypnosis; see Tart (1969, pp. 229–321), also Krippner (1968).

(4)   Group therapy experiences. This is essentially the basic encounter technique of Carl Rogers, which has many similarities to the closure of self-actualization. This process has been used by Schutz at Esalen, and by others in many other sections of the United States.

(5)   Random group pentacostal experiences, which may be of a patriotic, erotic, athletic or social nature as well as religious. Individual barriers are temporarily broken down, allowing for a feeling of euphoria and power.

Before going on to cognitive processes, the writer feels it necessary to direct two asides to the reader. The first is that the previous two sections are in outline form only, since this book is not a treatise on either drugs or mysticism. The second point is that the writer has grave doubts that artificial means to secure self-actualization do not cause more trouble than they cure. It is all well and fine to feel that one is in the throes of the greatest experience in the world, but two ounces of alcohol can sometimes accomplish the same trick. The question is: "What happens after the experience is over?" Is the cognitive part of the mind really changed so that the interactions of everyday life have become transformed?

As one whose attitudes are clearly biased against the use of drugs to induce psychedelia, the writer feels that one of the best psychological reasons which can be given is that the use of drugs in young people for this purpose is developmentally premature. Psychologists are agreed that for a child to wake up and see parents in the sexual act is not good for his developmental process. He is not ready for this knowledge which comes as a shock to him at this time, whereas there would be much less trauma in a similar situation at adolescence.

In the same way premature introduction to the experience of psychedelia while one is fighting the identity crisis or still in the throes of the sexual adjustment may be equally damaging and traumatic. Bucke (1929, p. 81) reported the average age of his "illumination" to be 36 years, well into the generativity period. And it is interesting to note that the earlier examples of illumination tend to be highly pyrotechnic, Pascal and Blake being two cases in point. Apparently bourbon whiskey is not the only thing that smoothes out with age. If a bridegroom needs an aphrodisiac on his wedding night, we may suspect that all is not well with his marriage; if another young person uses drugs to "turn on," we may wonder if he is not after thrills rather than self-actualization.

COGNITIVE TECHNIQUES FOR SELF-ACTUALIZATION

Self-actualization is a state of continual becoming in which one is thrown forward or caught up in the process of manifesting one's potentiality. While the process is heavily loaded with preconscious elements, it does appear that to some extent we can court the muse from the conscious side. To understand this mechanism it will be helpful again to review the process of creative openings from the preconscious.

Anyone who has experienced creative or psychedelic openings knows them to be far different from the more prosaic problem solving—for creative inspiration has a feeling quality all its own. It seems to fuse the Sullivanian uncanniness of the "not me" with the canniness of the me, which mutes the nightmare of the former into fantasy and elevates the pedestrianism of the latter into insight. The inspirational force accompanying this process is so strong that other sensory perceptions are dulled or stilled; ordinary biological drives such as hunger, thirst and excretion are forgotten; the individual is almost in a light hypnotic trance, paying complete attention to the inner voice. During this period of perceptual allay, a new flood of ideas, seemingly alien, come to mind so that it is all one can do to write them down. On such occasions, it appears as though one were taking down a message, striving to get it right, and being flooded with information which would be impossible to elicit at another time. Happy is he who under these circumstances is able to get all or most of the message on paper, for such openings are exceedingly difficult to recall and fade very rapidly.

Many people keep paper and pencil beside their beds so that if such inspiration comes at night they will be prepared. The scientist Loewi received such an opening about an important scientific formula and, when copying, forgot some of it. Fortunately, he was able to get the rest of it the next night in another dream.

Others have reported that such openings occur when they are released from tension such as on a vacation, in the presence of great natural beauty, after sexual intercourse, upon arising from sleep, upon hearing beautiful music, etc.

The main plan for this book, plus six pages of detailed notes, was taken down one Sunday afternoon at a hotel in Bali.

A creative opening is best conceptualized as a merging of the conscious and preconscious minds in which a flood of material previously cataloged by the conscious mind is reorganized by the preconscious and then expelled into the conscious domain. With the requisite conditions of mental health and environmental stimulation, the process seems inevitable, and a periodic function of mind at maturity.

A good place to look for a spring is near the spot where a mountain rises out of a plain, particularly where there is an outcrop of porous rock. Creativity is like a spring, issuing forth from the porous rock of the preconscious, under the hydrostatic pressure of the mountain of conscious accretion. A spring of fresh water often is a nuisance when it first develops, starting in as a muddy quagmire until the dirt and debris has cleared away and a channel has been dug for the runoff. But when this is done and the bedrock exposed, the spring will run clear and increase in volume and will become a source of life for all in the vicinity. Our problem is to transform that muddy quagmire into a flowing spring of life and creativity within ourselves.

Emerson (1950, p. 126) spoke of this very metaphor:

> When I watch that flowing river, out of regions I see not, pours for a season its streams into me, I see that I am a pensioner, not a cause, but a surprised spectator of this ethereal water; that I desire and look up and put myself in the attitude of reception, but from some alien energy the visions come.

Let us examine the problem of becoming personally more self-actualized as itself a step in creative problem-solving technique. A problem is an experience conceptualized in terms of its symptoms; an opportunity is an experience conceptualized in terms of its potentialities. Frequently the same experience can be turned from a problem to an opportunity by flexibility on our part in making this necessary but not always easy transformation. The first thing, then, is to try to arrange the problem from "in terms of symptoms" to "in terms of possibilities."

(1)   Many of us wish for good ideas, but often we do not recognize or nurture good ideas when they come. Creativity is not so much the having of good ideas as the process of nurturing them. Most of us are like some unfortunate women who find it easy to conceive but hard to carry to term; we continually get ideas, but we continually abort them. Often this is because the creative idea does not occur in a proper or "evening dress" form. Like most things just born, it needs to be nurtured, loved and cleaned up.

(2)   We need to develop a quiet time, when ordinary routine may be stripped away. In short, we need to court the muse. There are two rhythms here—a daily rhythm and a much longer one. There is sometime every day, usually around the time of sleep—just before or just after—when the gates to the preconscious seem to fall open. We should find out when this is best for us and cultivate it. Some people find music very helpful for this purpose; eventually it may be discovered that a light hypnotic trance may be useful; play and playful regression is

also desirable. The author, personally, finds water and swimming helpful, probably because it is relaxing.

The other rhythm is a much longer one of alternation of work and travel. The power to travel, especially outside one's culture, to evoke the creative response is sometimes almost unbelievable. This kind of alternation between work and a vacation is extremely useful.

(3)   Inevitably, in any creative functioning there will be a down cycle. The worst possible thing is to resist this tendency. Even a cow goes dry at times. Forcing will just result in the production of rubbish and in fouling the spring. The next worst thing at such a time is to resort to negative affective reactions or to believe that one is through. Hostility, resentment, envy, jealousy and other negative feelings dissipate the creative energy and result in destructive tendencies, often the self-destructive tendencies overtaking the creative ones.

To avoid this predicament, in the short term, one should seek nonhostile and nondestructive release of energy, consciously allowing oneself to play the feel or descend to the lowest level of slapstick enjoyment. Next to splashing around in a swimming pool the author finds that low-life comedy of the Laurel and Hardy or Abbott and Costello type is especially appropriate to the mood. One should not censor a rather immature and childlike regression in simple pleasures, such as going to circuses or watching inane antics of television. Whatever relaxes the individual in an innocent manner is enough.

On the long term, one should make a break with routine and travel abroad. Drastic change in one's living conditions is called for, and some methods for effecting this change have been detailed in the previous chapter.

(4)   A prosaic but helpful method is the single-minded study of the issue with all its opportunities and facets. A curious thing about this process is that, if you study ichthyology, you do not become more like a fish but, if you study creativity and self-actualization, you are very likely to become more creative and self-actualized. To some extent the openings between the conscious and the preconscious can be sprung a bit from the conscious side. This is a gradual process, but it should never be overlooked.

(5)   Kelly (1955) in his book on personal construct theory delivers a powerful axiom that the way we anticipate events constrains us to that type of experience of them. There is much psychological truth in this dictum which can be used to aid us in our search for self-actualization. Because we have been brought up to conform, we think we must eat, dress, talk and think like everyone else. Actually, our characters are formed and, indeed, our very lives molded by those things, events and persons to which we selectively give attention. We also tend to think of an individual "I" with its fears, greed and separatism, whereas we should think of group life as "bios" in which each individual has a connective part like branches on a tree. Life reaches for more creative perfection in individuals because only the individual has the capacity for self-actualization.

(6)   Another mode of change has to do with ceasing to live in the past and starting to live in the future. The process of creative functioning is that of manifesting the future (helping the inchoate future become manifest). This is the

real meaning of existentialism. The existential person is not bound by his past, for he is in a continual state of becoming in which he is thrown forward for definition into the future, and is better defined by what he may become than by what he is or was. When the writer gave his graduate students an assignment to write their own obituaries, he was surprised to find that there were those who seemed content to be killed tomorrow and had their funerals all figured out, but the more creative students thought of themselves as dying in the distant future after considerable escalation in their personal and professional lives.

The Hopi rain dance is danced to bring out or manifest the inner feelings and wishes for rain in the Hopi heart to actuality in the tribal experience. Our future indicative holds semantic traps. In using it (where most other cultures use the conditional), we ascribe reality and inevitability to the future, not recognizing that it is largely within our power to change it.

The key question is "Am I in control of my environment, or is my environment in control of me?" The creative person literally turns his dreams inside out; instead of being governed by them he is their master for he molds them and makes them come to pass. This possibility of intervention in one's future is characteristic of the self-actualized person. He sees future possibilities as inner realities and is able to make them actualities. Admittedly there are aspects of one's future over which one does not have control (such as the lack of control a mother has over the sex of her child), but just as the mother has much control over the health and, indeed, the life of the baby, so we have much control over future actuality because we can formulate our creative ideas. Many creative persons find that imagining pictures of things as one wishes them to be is helpful in making them more possible. First a trace, then a path, then a lane, finally a freeway. Or as Mark Twain said: "Everything goes through three stages: first people say it is impossible; then they say it conflicts with the Bible; finally they say they have always believed it."

Picturing in one's mind a desired end (such as seeing one arrive home after a long auto trip), as a means of creating or achieving, may seem dangerously near Coueism to some. But psychological investigation has increased our respect for the self-fulfilling prophecy. Such graphic representation of a future, even in one's mind, may set in motion many aids to reach that end (for example, in the case of the auto trip, one may drive more carefully). At any rate, if artists and architects picture their dreams first in their minds, then on paper, and finally in stone and steel, may not the rest of us recognize this as an effective procedure for realizing our dreams and wishes?

(7)   We need to purify our lives. This will be a pejorative statement for many but, after a careful search, the writer cannot find a word which better describes the function. The word is not used in reference to sexual abstinence, for that use seems merely to be an Anglo-Saxon "hang up." Rather, purity as we use it refers to the elimination of hostility, violence, filth and depravity from one's perceptual intake. While these matters roil up the mind, whether they come from movies, TV, or interpersonal contact, it cannot remain tranquil enough to receive the faint signals of creative ideas. For the mind is a receiver which must be powered so that it functions like a radio receiving set for picking up creative thoughts. A good set has high selection, and so does a self-actualized person.

Personal hostility in the family, among friends or in the office is extremely inimical to creative work. Even the atmosphere of hostility on a campus beset with unrest is enough to dampen most research progress. If one wishes to be creative, one must quiet the input from these areas so that one can march to the music of a distant drum.

Purification also involves the clearing up of lower order problems so that self-actualization, when it comes, will not be premature. The continually unsolved struggles of earlier tasks divert energy which should be channeled into new transformation. This is also one of the dangers of the use of drugs to achieve self-actualization.

(8) In preparing to be receptive to ideas, be sensitive to dissonance, discontinuity and small apertures. An aperture is a discontinuity in material which otherwise seems to fit well. But the aperture shows where the fit is less than perfect, and as Darwin said, it is the imperfections or flaws in the present theory which point to the genesis of the new or better theory. Our conceptualization of the world of experience is like so many stage flats, fitted together rather well, but with small apertures here and there (that is the only way we realize they are simulations of scenery and not scenery itself). By sensing the aperture, one gets a gestalt of the flat as distinct from the scenery it simulates; one is then on the road to reconceptualizing another scenery flat which will fit the position better without the discontinuity.

Apertures frequently appear as nuisance things (like the constant speed of light regardless of the emanating source), which one wishes would go away and about which one is not inclined to speculate (unless one is an Einstein). But if one wants to unravel the mystery, one had better start there and look for a loose thread. One pulls and pulls, and hopefully the thread does not give out until the knot is unraveled.

(9) The principles of psychotherapy are helpful in bringing groups or individuals from stasis into free flow and creativity; they can, hence, be used on some occasions for creative problem solving. We first get ourself and the participants to stop fighting the symptoms and each other and help them make an effort at more accurate communication. This means first learning to value one another. A "hostillectomy" session may be necessary where everybody gets out his gripes. Toward the end of this period, the group should be given two ideas: (1) the leader is capable of helping them to something new, and (2) they are capable of more ingenuity than they have shown in solving the problem.

Get them to look at the general mess from new angles. Often this involves brainstorming or a group-directed, day-dream session. Conducting it requires relaxation of rigid old type positions so some flux can take place. This activity is equivalent to the preliminary exploration in a therapeutic session. One gets as much personal identification into this stage as possible with no negative or pejorative evaluation.

It should not be possible to go through the classic aspects of creative problem solving, fact finding, problem finding, solution finding and acceptance finding. If resentment rises or arid spells occur, it may be necessary to go back to another group session to get things more in flux again. An exit session to bandage ego wounds and make maintenance of performance better may be desirable.

(10)   Among elementary methods sometimes found for inducing creativity are those which depend upon an automatic systematized run-down of possible actions (modify, adapt, magnify, minify, reverse, rearrange, combine) or a random juxtaposition of wildly unusual descriptive process (what happens when a political polecat meets a traumatized tiger in a Hungarian haberdashery?). These methods constitute a first step, to be sure, in eliciting fluency and flexibility in those who are strongly compartmentalized.

True creativity goes beyond this automatic feeding of raw stimuli directly to the conscious mind. A better method is illustrated by Torrance's "Sounds and Images" or Khatena's "Onomatopoeia and Images" (1969) in which material is absorbed while in a revery or when day dreaming or in a relaxed mode where it gets into the preconscious there to be transformed to verbal output, which is the product of the individual not the stimulator. The essence of the creative act lies in the focusing and transformation of energy. This can only come when the preconscious has a chance to organize the percept into a new form. Wordsworth in "To the Daffodils" illustrates both process and product when he tells us:

> And when upon my bed I lie
> In vacant or in pensive mood
> They flash upon the inward eye
> Which is the bliss of solitude.
> And then my heart with pleasure fills
> And dances with the daffodils.

(11)   A final hint has to do with the sensing of unnamed processes, entities or relationships. The concept of escalation in chapter 3 is such an example. Another illustration is the fact that New York comes before Newark alphabetically because the character between the W and the Y (which has no name, since it consists of space) comes before the letter A. These unnamed entities, processes and relations are found in every discipline and often perform major functions. They only await our discovery of them.

Some readers may be disappointed in the pedestrian nature of these modest suggestions. Others may point out that they apply more to creativity than to psychedelia or illumination. Yet creativity is the first level of self-actualization, and it is here that we must start. We must set this system in "go condition" if we expect the higher openings to take place. The preconscious is like the cave of Aladdin—full of treasures and guarded by a genie. We must be prepared to take advantage of both before we rub the lamp.

SUMMARY

Piaget once stated that the course of human development is a way from egocentricity toward freedom. Every aspect of life shows this upward escalation. For as all life strives upward, each individual life tries, however briefly, to become a god before it becomes an ape. For if man is the foetalization of the ape, differential psychology would point out that the ablest among men represent an even more youthful stretch-out of the plastic periods. This allows for the full eight stages (and perhaps more) to be included in our life span.

We start by trying to perfect in our developing brain an imperfect isomorphism between the external world and our concepts. If we progress to the end, keeping up environmental stimulation after the biological development has left off, we can become saint-like both cognitively and affectively. The mind first becomes capable of full representation of the external world, then merges with it in experience, finally to become part of the noumenon of that experience and so capable of influencing external events.

These are brave words, but man is a brave species. We may come from dust, but our destiny is in the stars. Thoreau, that rustic seer, closed *Walden* on a similar optimistic note, for speaking of the future of mankind he prophesied: "That day is yet to dawn, for the sun is only a morning star." And old Socrates told us the same thing long ago:

> For if the man had this power to contemplate beauty absolute, unfettered and untarnished by all the colors and vanities of human life, dwelling in that blissful realm alone, he would bring forth not images of beauty, but beauty itself, and so would become immortal and become the friend of the Gods.

Bibliography

Abdel-Salan, A. "Relationship between Selected Creativity Factors and Certain Non-intellectual Factors Among High School Students." (Unpub. doctoral dissertation.) Denver: University of Denver, 1963.

Adler, Alfred. *Problems of Neurosis*. London: Routledge, 1959.

Allport, G. W. *Patterns and Growth in Personality*. New York: Holt, Rinehart & Winston, 1961. p. 198.

Anderson, H. A. *Creativity and Its Cultivation*. New York: Harper Brothers, 1959.

Anderson, J. E. *Psychology of Development and Personal Adjustment*. New York: Henry Holt, 1949.

Anderson, J. E. *Psychological Aspects of Aging*. Washington: American Psychological Association, 1956.

Angyal, Andras. "A Theoretical Model for Personality Studies," in *The Self*, ed., C. E. Moustakas. New York: Harper & Row, 1956.

Arieti, S. *The Intrapsychic Self*. New York: Basic Books, 1967.

Arnold, J. E. "Creativity in Engineering," in *Creativity: An Examination of the Creative Process*, ed., P. Smith. New York: Hastings House, 1959.

Arnold, J. E. "The Generalist vs. the Specialist in Research and Development," pp. IX-X-13, in *The Creative Person*, ed., D. W. MacKinnon. Berkeley: University of California General Extension, 1962.

Aschner, M., and C. B. Bish. *Productive Thinking in Education.* Washington: National Education Association, 1965.

Atkinson, Bea. "Relationship between Problem-Solving Strategies and Measures of Convergent and Divergent Thinking in a Selected Group of Secondary School Students." (Unpub. doctoral dissertation.) Gainesville: University of Florida, 1964.

Barkan, M. *Through Art to Creativity.* Boston: Allyn & Bacon, 1960.

Barron, Frank. "Needs for Order and Disorder as Motives in Creative Activity," in *The Second Research Conference on the Identification of Creative Scientific Talent*, ed., C. W. Taylor. Salt Lake City: University of Utah Press, 1958.

Barron, Frank. *Creativity and Psychological Health.* New York: D. Van Nostrand, 1963.

Barron, Frank. *Creativity and Personal Freedom.* New York: D. Van Nostrand, 1968.

Bartlett, Frederick. *Thinking: An Experimental and Social Study.* New York: Basic Books, 1958.

Beggs, J. "Personality Changes at a Choice Point in Middle Life." (Unpub. doctoral dissertation.) Eugene, Ore.: University of Oregon, 1967.

Benton, J. E. "A Study of Relationships of Openness and Drive to Creativity," (67-10859) (Unpub. doctoral dissertation.) Tucson: Arizona State University, 1967.

Bergson, H. *Creative Evolution.* New York: Modern Library, 1944.

Besdine, M. "Mrs. Oedipus," pp. 103-8, in *Readings in Developmental Psychology Today*, ed., Phoebe Cramer. Del Mar, Cal.: Communications Research Machines Books, 1970.

Besdine, M. "The Jocasta Complex, Mothering and Genius." *Psychoanalytic Review*, 55:2, 1968.

Bjorksten, J. "The Limitation of Creative Years." *Scientific Monthly,* 62:94, 1946.

Blatt, S. J. "An Attempt to Define Mental Health." *Journal of Consulting Psychology*, 28:146–53, 1964.

Blocher, D. *Developmental Counseling.* New York: Ronald Press, 1966.

Bloom, B. S., and others. *Taxonomy of Educational Objectives, I, Cognitive Domain.* New York: McKay, 1956.

Bolk, Louis. *Das Problem des Menschenwerden.* Jena, Germany, 1926. (As used in J. B. S. Haldane. *The Causes of Evolution.* New York: Harper Brothers, 1932.)

Botwinick, J. *Cognitive Processes in Maturity and Old Age.* New York: Springer Publishing Co., 1967.

Bower, Eli G., and Hollister, W. G. *Behavioral Science Frontiers in Education.* New York: John Wiley & Sons, 1968.

Bowers, Patricia. "Effect of Hypnosis and Suggestions of Reduced Defensiveness on Creativity." (Unpub. doctoral dissertation.) Urbana: University of Illinois, 1965.

Brandwein, P. *The Gifted Student as a Future Scientist.* New York: Harcourt-Brace, 1955.

Brill, A. A. "Poetry as an Oral Outlet." *Psychoanalytic Review.* 18:4:357—78, October 1931.

Brown, Barbara. "Regulation of Aspects of Consciousness through Association with EEG Alpha Activity, Represented by a Light Signal." *Psychophysiology.* 6:442—52, 1970. (See also *Look*, 90:October 6, 1970.)

Bruner, J. "Inhelder and Piaget's: The Growth of Logical Thinking, a Psychologist's Viewpoint." *British Journal of Psychology*, 50:363—70, 1959.

Bruner, J. *On Knowing.* Cambridge, Mass.: Belknap Press, 1962.

Bruner, J. "The Conditions of Creativity," in *Contemporary Approaches to Creative Thinking*, ed., H. E. Gruber, G. Terrell, and M. Wertheimer. New York: Atherton Press, 1962.

Bruner, J. "The Creative Surprise," in *Contemporary Approaches to Creative Thinking*, ed., Gruber and others. New York: Atherton Press, 1962.

Bruner, J. *Toward a Theory of Instruction.* Cambridge, Mass.: Harvard University Press, 1966.

Bucke, R. M. *Cosmic Consciousness* (6th edition). New York: E. P. Dutton, 1929.

Buhler, Charlotte. *Varieties of Psychotherapy.* Glencoe, Ill.: Free Press, 1962.

Burt, C. "The Psychology of Creative Ability." *British Journal of Educational Psychology*, 32:292—98, 1969.

Burt, Cyril. "General Ability and Special Education," *Educational Research* (UK), 1:2:3—16, Feb. 1969.

Castelli, C. D. "An Exploration of the Relationship between Teacher Creative Ability and Teacher-Pupil Classroom Interaction." (Unpub. doctoral dissertation.) (64—13665), Buffalo: State University of New York, 1964.

Castiglione, L. V. "Relation of Intelligence to Selected Measures of Creativity." (66-9491) (Unpub. doctoral dissertation.) New York: New York University, 1965.

Chickering, A. W. *Education and Identity*. San Francisco: Jossey-Bass, 1969.

Conant, J. B. *The American High School Today*. New York: McGraw-Hill, 1959.

Condorcet, A. de. *Sketch for a Historical Picture of the Progress of the Human Mind*. (1795) (as cited in Hardin's *Nature and Man's Fate*, 1961.) New York: Noonday Press, 1955.

Coone, J. G. "Cross Cultural Study of Sex Difference in the Development of Selected Creative Thinking Abilities." *Dissertation Abstracts*, 29:4828, 1968.

Craig, R. H. "Traits, Tests and Creativity." *Psychologia: International Journal of Psychology*, 9:107–10, 1966.

Cropley, A. J. "Originality, Intelligence and Personality." (Unpub. doctoral dissertation.) Alberta, Can.: University of Alberta, 1965.

Damm, V. J. "Creativity and Intelligence: Research Implications for Equal Emphasis in High School." *Exceptional Children*, 36:565–70, April 1970.

Datta, L. E. and Parloff, M. R. "On the Relevance of Autonomy: Parent-Child Relationships and Early Scientific Creativity." *Proceedings of the 75th Annual Convention of the American Psychological Association.* 2:149–50, 1967. (*Psych. Abstracts*, 1967:13452.)

Decarie, Therese. *Intelligence and Affectivity in Early Childhood*. New York: International Universities Press, 1965.

Denny, D. A. "A Preliminary Analysis of an Observation Schedule Designed to Identify the Teacher-Classroom Variables Which Facilitate Pupil Creative Growth." (Unpub. doctoral dissertation.) Bloomington: University of Indiana, 1966.

Deri, F. "On Sublimation." *Psychoanalytic Quarterly*, 8:3:325–34, 1939.

Deutsch, M., I. Katz and A. Jensen. *Social Class, Race and Psychological Development*. New York: Holt, Rinehart & Winston, 1968.

Dever, W. T. "Relationship between Creative Thinking Ability of Selected Fourth Graders and Parental Attitudes." (65-4879) (Unpub. doctoral dissertation.) Denton: North Texas State University, 1964.

Dewey, John. *How We Think*. Boston: D. C. Heath, 1910.

Dinkmeyer, D. C., and C. E. Caldwell. *Developmental Counseling and Guidance*. New York: McGraw-Hill, 1970.

Edwards, M. O. "A Survey of Creative Problem-Solving Courses." *Journal of Creative Behavior*, 2:33–35, 1968.

Ehrenzweig, Anton. *The Psychoanalysis of Artistic Vision and Hearing*. London: Routledge, 1953.

Elkind, D., and J. H. Flavel. *Studies in Cognitive Development: Essays in Honor of Jean Piaget*. New York: Oxford University Press, 1969.

Ellenger, Bernice, "The Home Environment and the Creative Thinking Abilities of Children." (Unpub. doctoral dissertation.) Columbus: Ohio State University, 1964.

Emerson, Ralph Waldo. *Selected Prose and Poetry*. New York: Rinehart, 1950.

Engleman, A. A. "A Case of Transexion upon Viewing a Painting." *American Image*, 9:239–49, 1952.

Erikson, E. "The Eight Stages of Man," in *Childhood and Society* (2d edition). New York: Norton, 1963.

Erikson, E. *Insight and Responsibility*. New York: W. W. Norton, 1964.

Erikson, E. H. *Ghandi's Truth: On the Origin of Militant Non-violence*. New York: W. W. Norton, 1969.

Escalona, S. K. *The Roots of Individuality*. Chicago: Aldine, 1968.

Evans, R. I. *Dialog with Erik Erikson*. New York: Harper & Row, 1967.

Fairbairn, W. R. D. "Prolego Mena to a Psychology of Art." *British Journal of Psychology*, 28:288–303, 1938.

Feld, S. "Creative Potential, Intelligence and the Heil-Sheviko Personality Profiles." *Dissertation Abstracts*, 28:12A:4906–7, 1968.

Flavell, John H. *The Developmental Psychology of Jean Piaget*. New York: Van Nostrand, 1963.

Flax, M. L. "Stability of Relationship between Creativity and Personality Variables." (Unpub. doctoral dissertation.) Fort Collins: Colorado State University, 1966.

Fliegler, L. A. *Curriculum Planning for the Gifted*. Englewood Cliffs, N. J.: Prentice-Hall, 1961.

Ford, D. H., and H. B. Urban. *Systems of Psychotherapy*. New York: John Wiley & Co., 1963.

Foster, Florence. "The Human Relationships of Creative Individuals." *Journal of Creative Behavior*, 2:111–18, Spring 1968.

Freud, S. *Leonardo Da Vinci: A Study in Psychosexuality (1910)*. New York: Random House, 1947.

Fried, Edrita. *Artistic Productivity and Mental Health*. Springfield, Ill.: C. C. Thomas Co., 1964.

Frierson, E. C. "A Study of Selected Characteristics of Gifted Children from Upper and Lower Socio-economic Backgrounds." (67-9821) (Unpub. doctoral dissertation.) Kent, Ohio: Kent State University, 1964.

Fromm, Erich. "The Creative Attitude," in *Creativity and Its Cultivation*, ed. by Harold H. Anderson. New York: Harper & Row, 1959.

Furth, H. G. *Piaget and Knowledge*. Englewood Cliffs, N. J.: Prentice-Hall, 1969.

Galton, F. *Hereditary Genius*. London: Macmillan & Co., 1869.

Galton, F. *Inquiries into Human Faculty and Its Development*. London: Dent, 1883.

Gerard, Ralph W. "What is Imagination?" in *Selected Readings on the Learning Process*, ed. by T. L. Harris and W. E. Schwan. New York: Oxford University Press, 1961.

Gerber, B. W. A. "A Study of the Relationship between Psychological Health and Creativity." *Dissertation Abstracts*, 15:(10):5733, 1965.

Getzels, J. W., and P. W. Jackson. *Creativity and Intelligence*. New York: John Wiley & Sons, 1962.

Ghiselin, Brewster (ed). *The Creative Process*. New York: New American Library, 1952.

Ghiselin, Brewster. "Ultimate Criteria for Two Levels of Creativity," in *The Second University of Utah Research Conference on the Identification of Creative Scientific Talent (1957)*, ed. by C. W. Taylor. Salt Lake City: University of Utah Press, 1959.

Goertzel, V., and M. G. Goertzel. *Cradles of Eminence*. Boston: Little, Brown, 1962.

Goralski, Patricia. "Creativity: Student Teachers Perceptions of Approaches to Classroom Teaching." (Unpub. doctoral dissertation.) Minneapolis: University of Minnesota Press, 1964.

Gordon, W. J. *Synectics: The Development of Creative Capacity*. New York: Harper, 1961.

Gowan, J. C., and G. D. Demos. *Education and Guidance of the Ablest*. Springfield, Ill.: C. C. Thomas, 1964.

Gowan, J. C., and G. D. Demos (eds). *The Guidance of Exceptional Children.* New York: McKay, 1965.

Gowan, J. C. "Creativity and Cognitive Competence." *Gifted Child Quarterly,* 9:6–9, Spring 1965.

Gowan, J. C. "What Makes a Gifted Child Creative: Four Theories." *Gifted Child Quarterly,* 9:3–6, Spring 1965.

Gowan, J. C., and G. D. Demos. "The Counselor and the Creative Child." *The Gifted Child Quarterly,* 9:184–6, Winter 1965.

Gowan, J. C. and E. P. Torrance. "An Intercultural Study of Non-verbal Ideational Fluency." *Gifted Child Quarterly,* 9:13–16, Spring 1965.

Gowan, J. C., and G. D. Demos. *The Disadvantaged and Potential Dropout: Compensatory Educational Programs.* Springfield, Ill.: C. C. Thomas, 1966.

Gowan, J. C. "Managing the Post-partum Depression in Creative Persons." *Gifted Child Quarterly,* 11:90–2, Summer 1967.

Gowan, J. C. "Issues in the Guidance of Gifted and Creative Students." *Gifted Child Quarterly,* 11:2:140–4, Autumn 1967.

Gowan, J. C., and C. B. Bruch. "What Makes a Creative Person a Creative Teacher?" *Gifted Child Quarterly,* 11:157–59, Autumn 1967.

Gowan, J. C., G. D. Demos and E. P. Torrance (eds). *Creativity: Its Educational Implications.* New York: John Wiley, 1967.

Gowan, J. C. "The Guidance of Creative Children." *Journal of Women Deans and Counselors,* 31:154–61, Summer 1968.

Gowan, J. C. "How Parents Can Foster Creativity in Their Children." in *Reaching for Creative Endeavor: Bold New Venture,* ed. by W. Michael. Bloomington: Indiana University Press, 1968.

Gowan, J. C. "Developmental Process and Its Guidance Implications." *California Personnel and Guidance Association Journal,* 1:18–22, Winter 1968–69.

Gowan, J. C. "Why Some Gifted Children are Creative," *Gifted Child Quarterly,* 15:13–19, Spring 1971.

Gray, J. J. "An Investigation of the Relation between Primary Process Thinking and Creativity." (Fordham, 1967). *Dissertation Abstracts,* 28:12B–5206, 1968.

Greenacre, P. "The Childhood of the Artist." *Psychoanalytic Study of the Child,* 12:47–52, 1957.

Greenacre, P. "Discussion and Comments on the Psychology of Creativity." *Journal of the American Academy of Child Psychiatry*, 1:108—28, 1962.

Grotjohan, M. *Beyond Laughter.* New York: McGraw-Hill, 1957.

Guilford, J. P. "Creativity." *American Psychologist*, 5:444—54, 1950.

Guilford, J. P. "Three Faces of Intellect." *American Psychologist*, 14:469—79, 1959.

Guilford, J. P. "Traits of Creativity," pp. 142—61 in *Creativity and Its Cultivation,* ed. by H. A. Anderson. New York: Harper Brothers, 1959.

Guilford, J. P. "A Psychometric Approach to Creativity" (mimeo). Los Angeles, Calif.: University of Southern California, 1962.

Guilford, J. P. *The Nature of Human Intelligence.* New York: McGraw-Hill, 1967.

Guilford, J. P. "Frames of Reference for Creative Behavior in the Arts," pp. 189—95, in *Creativity: Its Educational Implications*, ed. by J. C. Gowan and others. New York: John Wiley & Co., 1967.

Guth, R. O. "Creativity, Competitive Drive and Interest Patterns Associated with Success in a Program for Academically Talented High School Students." (Unpub. doctoral dissertation.) Philadelphia: Temple University, 1966.

Hadamard, J. *The Psychology of Invention in the Mathematical Field.* New York: Dover Publications, 1954.

Hadley, D. J. "Experimental Relationships between Creativity and Anxiety." (Unpub. doctoral dissertation.) Ann Arbor: University of Michigan, 1965.

Haimowitz, M. L., and N. R. Haimowitz. *Human Development (A Book of Readings).* New York: Crowell Publishing Co., 1960.

Hallman, R. J. "The Necessary and Sufficient Conditions of Creativity," *Journal of Humanistic Psychology*, 3:1, Spring 1963. (Also reprinted in J. C. Gowan and others, *Creativity: Its Educational Implications.* New York: John Wiley & Co., 1967.)

Hallman, R. J. "Aesthetic Pleasure and the Creative Process." *Journal of Humanistic Psychology*, 6:2:141—48, Fall 1966.

Hallman, R. J. "Techniques of Creative Teaching." *Journal of Creative Behavior, I,* Sept. 1966.

Happich, C. "Das Bildbe Wusstein als Ansatzstelle Psychscher Behandlung." *Zbl. Psychotherapy*, 5:663—77, 1932.

Hardin, G. *Nature and Man's Fate.* New York: Mentor Books, 1961.

Harding, R. E. M. *An Anatomy of Genius.* London, 1942.

Hart, H. H. "The Integrative Function in Creativity." *Psychiatric Quarterly,* 24:1:1–16, 1950.

Helder, J. "Flexibility and Rigidity of Perceptual-cognitive Constructs: A Study of Creative States of Awareness." *Dissertation Abstracts,* 29:3467, 1968.

Helson, R. "Personality of Women with Imaginative and Artistic Interests: The Role of Masculinity, Originality and Other Characteristics in Their Creativity." *Personality,* 34:1–25, 1966.

Helson, R. "Personality Characteristics and Developmental History of Creative College Women." *Genetic Psychology Monographs,* 76:205–56, 1967. (See also "Sex Differences in Creative Styles." *Personality,* 35:214–33, 1967.)

Higgins, D. A. "Student Decision Making and Vocational Development: A Review of the Literature," in *Interim Report Project 6-1830: A Study of Intellectual Growth and Vocational Development,* ed. by T. L. Hilton. Princeton: Educational Testing Service, 1967.

Hilgard, E. R. "Creativity and Problem-Solving," in *Creativity and Its Cultivation,* ed. by H. A. Anderson. New York: Harper Brothers, 1959.

Hitschmann, E. *Great Men.* New York: International University Press, 1956.

Horonton, C. "Creativity and Precognition Scoring Level." *Journal of Parapsychology,* 31:29–42, 1967.

Hunt, J. McV. *Intelligence and Experience.* New York: Ronald Press, 1961.

Hurlock, E. *Child Development.* New York: McGraw-Hill, 1956.

Hutchinson, E. D. *How to Think Creatively.* Nashville: Abingdon Press, 1949.

Huxley, Aldous. *The Doors of Perception.* New York: Harper & Row, 1964a.

Huxley, Aldous. *Heaven and Hell.* New York: Harper & Row, 1964b.

Irving, D. J. "An Empirical Study between Certain Pupil Characteristics and Selected Measures of Creativity." (Unpub. doctoral dissertation.) Chapel Hill: University of North Carolina, 1963.

Isaacs, S. *Intellectual Growth in Young Children.* New York: Schocken Books, 1966.

Jackson, P. W. and Messick, S. "The Person, the Product, and the Response: Conceptual Problems in the Assessment of Creativity," *Personality,* 33:309–329, 1965.

James, W. *The Varieties of Religious Experience.* New York: New American Library, 1958. (First printed, 1902.)

Jenkins, J. M. "A Study of the Characteristics Associated with Innovative Behavior in Teachers." (Unpub. doctoral dissertation.) Miami, Ohio: University of Miami, 1967.

Jourard, S. M. "Growing Awareness and the Awareness of Growth," p. 2, in *Ways of Growth*, ed. by H. Otto and J. Mann. New York: Viking Press, 1968.

Jung, C. G. *Psychology of the Unconscious*, trans. by B. M. Hinkle. New York: Dodd, Mead, 1916.

Katz, J. and others. *No Time for Youth*. San Francisco: Jossey-Bass, Inc., 1969.

Kelly, George. *Psychology of Personal Constructs*. New York: W. W. Norton, 1955.

Khatena, J. and J. C. Gowan. "Crosscultural Measurement of Intelligence with DAM and RPM." *Gifted Child Quarterly*, 11:227–30, Winter 1967.

Khatena, J. "Onomatopoeia and Images." *Perceptual and Motor Skills*, 28:335–38, 1969.

Kinsey, A. C., and others. *Sexual Behavior in the Human Male*. Philadelphia: W. B. Saunders, 1948.

Klee, P. *Paul Klee on Modern Art* (with introduction by Herbert Read). London: Faber and Faber, 1966.

Kneller, G. F. *The Art and Science of Creativity*. New York: Holt, Rinehart and Winston, 1965.

Koestler, A. *The Act of Creation*. London: Hutchinson, 1964.

Kovell, K., and J. B. Shields. "Some Aspects of a Study of the Gifted Child." *British Journal of Educational Psychology*, 37:2:201, June 1967.

Krathwohl, D. R., B. S. Bloom and B. B. Masia. *Taxonomy of Educational Objectives: Handbook II: Affective Domain*. New York: McKay, 1964.

Krippner, S. "The Psychedelic State, the Hypnotic Trance and the Creative Act." *Journal of Humanistic Psychology*, 8:49–67, 1968.

Kris, E. *Psychoanalytic Exploration in Art*. New York: International University Press, 1952.

Kris, E. "Psychoanalysis and the Study of Creative Imagination." *Bulletin of N. Y. Academy of Medicine*, 334–51, 1953.

Kubie, L. *Neurotic Distortion of the Creative Process*. Lawrence: University of Kansas Press, 1958.

Kubie, L.S. "Unsolved Problems of Scientific Education." *Daedalus*, 94:3:564–87, Summer 1965.

Kubie, L. S. "Blocks to Creativity," pp. 33–43, in *Explorations in Creativity*, ed. by R. L. Mooney and T. A. Razik. New York: Harper & Row, 1967.

Lehman, H. C. *Age and Achievement*. Princeton: Princeton University Press, 1953.

Lehman, H. C. "The Age Decrement in Outstanding Scientific Creativity." *American Psychologist*, 15:128–34, Feb. 1960.

Levey, H. B. "A Theory Concerning Free Creation in the Inventive Arts." *Psychiatry*, 2:2:229–231, May 1940.

Lieberman, J. Nina. "The Relationship between Playfulness and Divergent Thinking at the Kindergarten Level." *Journal of Genetic Psychology*, 107:219–24, 1965.

Lieberman, J. Nina. "A Developmental Analysis of Playfulness as a Clue to Cognitive Style." *Journal of Creative Behavior*, 1:391–97, 1967.

Loevinger, Jane, and Ruth Wessler. *Measuring Ego Development*. San Francisco: Jossey-Ball, 1970.

Longfellow, H. W. "Nature," in *The Complete Poems of H. W. Longfellow*. Boston: Houghton-Mifflin Co., 1922.

Lowen, Alex O. *Pleasure*. New York: Coward-McCann, 1970.

Lowenfeld, V. "Current Research on Creativity." *Journal of the National Educational Association*, 47:538–40, 1958.

Luker, W. A. "Relationship between Personality Variables and Creativity." (Unpub. doctoral dissertation.) Denton: North Texas State University, 1963.

Macalpine, I., and R. Hunter. "Rossini: Piano Pieces for the Primal Scene," *American Imago*, 9:213–19, 1952.

MacKinnon, D. W. "Creativity and Images of the Self," in *The Study of Lives*, ed. by R. W. White. New York: Atherton, 1966.

MacKinnon, D. W. "The Nature and Nurture of Creative Talent," pp. 305–23, in *Readings in Learning and Human Abilities*, ed. by R. E. Ripple. New York: Harper & Row, 1964.

Mack, J. E. *Nightmares and Human Conflict*. Boston: Little, Brown Co., 1970.

Mackler, B. "Creativity and Life Styles." (Unpub. doctoral dissertation.) Lawrence: University of Kansas, 1962.

Maier, H. W. *Three Theories of Child Development*. New York: Harper & Row, 1965.

Maier, N. F. R. "Reasoning and Learning." *Psychological Review,* 38:322–46, 1931. (See also *Journal of Comparative Psychology*, 12:181–94, 1931.)

Maier, N. F. R. "Leadership Principles for Problem-Solving Conferences," in *Problem-Solving and Creativity*, ed. by the author. Belmont, Cal.: Brook Cole Publishing Co., 1970.

Margolies, A., and Sheldon Litt. "Creativity in Art: A Bioenergetic Approach," *Journal of Humanistic Psychology*, 6:148–55, 1966.

Mascolo, R. P. "Key Conceptual Schemes and Inquiry Training: Some Effects upon New Learning." (Unpub. doctoral dissertation.) New York: New York University, 1967.

Maslow, A. *Motivation and Personality.* New York: Harper Brothers, 1954.

Maslow, A. H. "Personality Problems and Personality Growth," pp. 323–46, in *The Self*, ed. by C. E. Moustakas. New York: Harper & Row, 1956.

Maslow, A. H. "Emotional Blocks to Creativity," *Journal of Individual Psychology*, 14:51–56, 1958.

Maslow, A. H. "Creativity in Self-Actualizing People," pp. 83–95, in *Creativity and Its Cultivation*, ed. by H. A. Anderson. New York: Harper Brothers, 1959.

Maslow, A. H. *Toward a Psychology of Being.* Princeton: D. Van Nostrand, 1962.

Maslow, A. H. "The Creative Attitude," in *Explorations in Creativity*, ed. by R. L. Mooney and T. A. Razik. New York: Harper & Row, 1967.

Massialas, B. G., and J. Zevin. *Creative Encounters in the Classroom.* New York: John Wiley & Co., 1967.

Masters, R. E. L., and J. Houston. *The Varieties of Psychedelic Experience.* New York: Holt, Rinehart and Winston, 1966.

McClelland, D. C. *Personality.* New York: William Sloane, 1951.

McGuire, C., E. Hindsman, F. J. King and E. Jennings. "Dimensions of Talented Behavior." *Educational and Psychological Measurement*, 21:3–38, 1961.

McKellar, Peter. *Imagination and Thinking.* New York: Basic Books, 1957.

McNeil, T. F. "The Relationship between Creative Ability and Recorded Mental Illness." *Dissertation Abstracts*, 30:5B:2604, 1969.

Mednick, S. A. "The Associative Basis of Creativity," *Psychology Review*, 69:220–32, 1962.

Meier, N.C. "Factors in Artistic Aptitude," *Psychology Monograph*, 51:5:140–58, 1939.

Miller, G. H. "An Investigation of Teacher Behavior and Pupil Thinking." (Unpub. doctoral dissertation.) Salt Lake City: University of Utah, 1964.

Montmasson, J. M. *Invention and the Unconscious.* London: K. Paul, French and Trubner, 1931.

Mooney, R. L. "Groundwork for Creative Research," pp. 261—70, in *The Self*, ed. by C. E. Moustakas. New York: Harper & Row, 1956.

Mooney, R. L., and T. A. Razik (eds). *Explorations in Creativity.* New York: Harper & Row, 1967.

Moriarty, A., and G. Murphy. "Some Thoughts about—Creativity and Paranormal Experience." *Journal of the American Society for Psychic Research*, 61:203—15, 1967.

Morris, C. W. *Varieties of Human Values.* Chicago: University of Chicago Press, 1956.

Moustakas, C. *Creativity and Conformity.* New York: Van Nostrand Reinhold Co., 1967.

Murphy, Gardner. *Human Potentialities.* New York: Basic Books, Inc., 1958.

Murray, H. S. "Vicissitudes of Creativity," pp. 96—118, in *Creativity and Its Cultivation*, ed. by H. A. Anderson. New York: Harper Bros., 1959.

Myers, F. W. *Human Personality and Its Survival after Death.* London, 1903.

Neugarten, B. *Personality in Middle and Late Life.* New York: Atherton Press. 1964.

Newfield, J. J. "Relationship of Creative Thinking Abilities to Academic Achievement of Adolescents." (Unpub. doctoral dissertation.) Denver: University of Denver, 1964.

Newton, R. C. "The Relation between Self-actualization and Educational Level" (Washington State U., 1968). *Dissertation Abstracts*, 29:5A:1453, 1968.

Nietzsche, F. *Ecce Homo: The Philosophy of Nietzsche.* New York: Modern Library, 1927.

Orinstein, A. S. "An Investigation of Parental-Child Rearing Attitudes and Creativity in Children." (Unpub. doctoral dissertation.) Denver: University of Denver, 1961.

Osborn, A. *Applied Imagination.* New York: Scribner's, 1953.

Otto, Herbert A., and John Mann. *Ways of Growth: Approaches to Expanding Awareness.* New York: Viking Press, 1969.

Owens, R. E. "The Relationship of Creative Thinking Abilities to Extreme Over-and-Under Achievement." (Unpub. doctoral dissertation.) Greeley: Colorado State College, 1964.

Pang, H., and L. Fort. "Relatedness of Creativity . . . and ESP." *Perceptual and Motor Skills*, 24:650, 1967.

Pankove, Ethel. "Relationship between Creativity and Risk-taking in V Grade Children." (Unpub. doctoral dissertation.) New Brunswick, N. J.: Rutgers University, 1966.

Patrick, Catherine. "Creative Thought in Artists." *Journal of Psychology*, 4:35—73, January 1937.

Patton, Cora. "Divergent Thinking and Language in Nursery School Children." (Unpub. doctoral dissertation.) Tallahassee: Florida State University, 1965.

Paul, W. J. "Psychological Characteristics of the Innovator." (Unpub. doctoral dissertation.) Cleveland: Western Reserve University, 1965.

Perkins, S. A. "A Comparative Analysis of the Congruence of High Creative and Low Creative High School Students." (66-12979) (Unpub. doctoral dissertation.) Eugene, Ore.: University of Oregon, 1966.

Piaget, J. *The Psychology of Intelligence*. London: Routledge and Kegan Paul, 1950.

Piaget, J. *Play Dreams and Imitation in Childhood*. London: Routledge and Kegan Paul, 1951.

Pinard, A., and M. Laurendeau. "Stage in Piaget's Cognitive Development Theory: Exegesis of a Concept," pp. 121—70, in *Studies in Cognitive Development*, ed. by D. Elkind and J. H. Flavell. New York: Oxford University Press, 1969.

Poincare, H. *The Foundations of Science*. New York: Science Press, 1913.

Rank, Otto. *Art and the Artist*. New York: Tudor Publishing Co., 1932.

Reich, C. A. *The Greening of America*. New York: Random House, 1970.

Roe, A. "Psychological Approaches to Creativity in Science," pp. 153—182 in *Essays on Creativity in the Sciences*, ed. by M. A. Coler. New York: New York University Press, 1963.

Roe, Anne. "Early Determinants of Vocational Choice," *Journal of Counseling Psychology*, 4:212—7, 1957.

Rogers, Carl R. "Toward a Theory of Creativity," pp. 69—82, in *Creativity and Its Cultivation*, ed. by H. A. Anderson. New York: Harper Bros., 1959.

Rogers, Carl R. *On Becoming a Person.* Boston: Houghton-Mifflin Co., 1961.

Rossman, J. *The Psychology of the Inventor.* Washington: Inventors Publishing Co., 1931.

Ruitenbeek, H. M. *The Creative Imagination.* New York: Quadrangle Press, 1965.

Sadler, W. A., Jr. "Creative Existence: Play as a Pathway to Personal Freedom." *Humanitas*, 5:57—80, Spring 1969.

Samson, R. W., and W. Upton. *Creative Analysis.* New York: E. P. Dutton, 1961.

Samson, R. W. *The Mind Builder.* New York: E. P. Dutton, 1965.

Saveca, A. F. "The Effects of Reward, Race, I.Q. and Socio-economic Status on Creativity in Preschool Children." (Unpub. doctoral dissertation.) Baton Rouge, La.: Louisiana State University, 1965.

Schactel, E. C. "The Development of Focal Attention and the Emergence of Reality." *Psychiatry*, 17:4:309—24, Nov. 1954.

Schactel, E. C. *Metamorphosis.* New York: Basic Books, Inc., 1959.

Schaefer, Charles E. "A Psychological Study of 10 Exceptionally Creative Adolescent Girls." *Exceptional Children* 36:6, Feb. 1970.

Schaeffer, E. S., and R. O. Bell. "Development of a Parent Attitude Research Instrument." *Child Development*, 29:339—61, 1958.

Schneider, D. E. *The Psychoanalyst and the Artist.* New York: Farrar-Strauss, 1950.

Schrodinger, E. *What Is Life?* Cambridge, Mass.: Cambridge University Press, 1944.

Schulman, D. "Openness of Perception as a Condition for Creativity." *Exceptional Children*, 33:89—94, 1966.

Sears, Pauline S. "A Study of Development of Creativity: Research Problems in Parental Antecedents," pp. 217 ff, in *Creativity at Home and School*, ed. by F. E. Williams. St. Paul: Macalester College Creativity Project, 1968.

Sears, R. R., and others. *Patterns of Child Rearing.* New York: Harper and Row, 1957.

Sechi, V. "Creativity and Kierkegaard." *Humanitas*, 5:81—98, Spring 1969.

Segal, Hanna. "A Psychoanalytic Approach to Aesthetics." *International Journal of Psychoanalysis*, 33:196—207, 1952.

Sharpe, Ella. "Certain Aspects of Sublimation and Delusion." *International Journal of Psychoanalysis*, 11:12—23, 1930.

Sheldon, W. T. *Varieties of Human Physique.* New York: Harper Bros., 1940.

Sheldon, W. T. *Varieties of Temperament.* New York: Harper Bros., 1942.

Sheldon, W. T. *Varieties of Delinquent Youth.* New York: Harper Bros., 1949.

Shostrom, E. L. *Manual for the Personal Orientation Inventory.* San Diego: Educational and Industrial Testing Service, 1966.

Sidle, A. C. "Creativity and Delusional Thinking in Schizophrenics." (67-7971) (Unpub. doctoral dissertation.) Palo Alto: Stanford University, 1967.

Simon, W., and J. Gagnon. "Psychosexual Development." *Transaction,* 6:5:9–18, March 1969.

Singer, J. L. "Imagination and Writing in Young Children." *Journal of Personality,* 29:396–413, 1961.

Sinott, E. W. "The Creativeness of Life," pp. 12–29, in *Creativity and Its Cultivation,* ed. by H. A. Anderson. New York: Harper Bros., 1959.

Skinner, B. F. "Why Teachers Fail." *Saturday Review,* 80, Oct. 16, 1965.

Smith, Robert H. "A Study of Pre-adolescent Boys Demonstrating Various Levels of Creativity with Regard to Their Social Adjustment, Peer-acceptance, and Academically Related Behavior." (Unpub. doctoral dissertation.) Denton, Tex.: North Texas State University, 1964.

Solomon, A. B. (American U., 1968). "A Comparative Analysis of Creativity and Intelligent Behavior of Elementary School Children with Different Socioeconomic Backgrounds." *Dissertation Abstracts,* 29:7A:145, 1968.

Spearman, C. *The Abilities of Man.* London: Macmillan, 1927.

Spearman, C. *The Creative Mind.* New York: Appleton-Century Crofts, 1931.

Spender, S. "The Making of a Poem." *Partisan Review,* 13:3:294–308, Summer 1946.

Spock, Benjamin. *Decent and Indecent.* New York: McCall Pub. Co., 1970.

Stein, M. I. "Creativity and Culture." *Journal of Psychology,* 36:311–22, Oct. 1953.

Sterba, R., and E. Sterba. "Beethoven and His Nephew." *International Journal of Psychoanalysis,* 33:470–78, 1952.

Stevenson, R. L. *Across the Plains.* New York: Scribner, 1909.

Stewart, K. "The Senoi," pp. 159 ff, in *Altered States of Consciousness,* ed. by H. H. Tart. New York: John Wiley Co., 1969.

Stiteville, J. R. "Life History Patterns of Highly Creative Inventors" (UCLA, 1966). *Dissertation Abstracts*, 27:11A:3551–2, 1967.

Sullivan, H. S. *The Interpersonal Theory of Psychiatry*. New York: W. W. Norton, 1953.

Taft, Ronald. "Creativity Hot and Cold" (mimeo). Melbourne, Aus.: Monash University, 1970.

Tart, C. T. (ed). *Altered States of Consciousness*. New York: John Wiley & Sons, 1969.

Taylor, C. W., and J. L. Holland. "Development and Application of Tests of Creativity." *Review of Educational Research*, 32:91–102, 1962.

Taylor, C. W., and Frank Barron (eds). *Scientific Creativity: Its Recognition and Development*. New York: John Wiley & Sons, 1963.

Taylor, C. W. (ed). *Creativity: Progress and Potential*. New York: McGraw-Hill and Co., 1964.

Taylor, C. W. "Clues to Creative Thinking," in *Creativity: Its Educational Implications*, ed by J. C. Gowan. New York: John Wiley & Sons, 1967.

Taylor, I. A. "The Nature of the Creative Process," pp. 51–82, in *Creativity: An Examination of the Creative Process*, ed. by E. P. Smith. New York: Hastings House, 1959.

Terman, L. M. *Genetic Studies of Genius*. Vol. I. Palo Alto: Stanford University Press, 1925.

Terman, L. M., and M. H. Oden. *The Gifted Child Grows Up: Twenty-five Years' Follow-up of a Superior Group*. London: Oxford University Press, 1947.

Thomson, R. *The Psychology of Learning*. Baltimore: Penguin Books (A453), 1959.

Thorndike, E. L. "Some Methodological Issues in the Study of Creativity," pp. 436–45, in *Testing Problems in Perspective: 25th Anniversary Volume: Topical Readings of the Annual Conference on Testing Problems*, ed. by A. Anastasi. Washington: American Council on Education, 1966.

Thorndike, R. L. "The Measurement of Creativity." *Teachers College Board*, 64:422–24, 1963.

Tibbetts, J. W. (USC, 1968). "The Relation between Socio-economic Status, Race, Sex, Intelligence, Age and Grade Point Average to Creativity in Adolescence." *Dissertation Abstracts*, 29:4A:1174, 1968.

Torrance, E. P. *Guiding Creative Talent*. Englewood Cliffs, N. J.: Prentice-Hall, 1962.

Torrance, E. P. *Rewarding Creative Behavior.* Englewood Cliffs, N. J.: Prentice-Hall, 1964.

Torrance, E. P. *Gifted Children in the Classroom.* New York: Macmillan and Co., 1965.

Torrance, E. P. "What is Honored . . . : Comparative Studies of Creative Achievement and Motivation." *Journal of Creative Behavior,* 3:149–54, Summer 1969.

Torrance, E. P., J. C. Gowan, J. J. Wu and N. Aliotti. "Creative Functioning of Monolingual and Bilingual Children in Singapore." *Journal of Educational Psychology,* 61:72–7, 1970.

Tyrrell, G. N. M. *The Personality of Man.* West Drayton, Eng.: Pelican Books (A165), 1947.

Upton, A. *Creative Analysis.* New York: E. P. Dutton, 1961.

Van Deren, R. H. "Development of Selected Creative Thinking Abilities through Creative Discussion of the Seventh Grade Curriculum." (Unpub. doctoral dissertation.) Los Angeles: University of Southern California, 1967.

Van der Sterren, H. A. "The 'King Oedipus' of Sophocles." *International Journal of Psychoanalysis,* 33:343–50, 1952.

Vernon, P. E. "Creativity and Intelligence." *Journal of Educational Research,* 6:163–69, 1964.

Vinacke, W. E. *The Psychology of Thinking.* New York: McGraw-Hill, 1952.

Walberg, H. L. "Physics Femininity and Creativity." *Developmental Psychology,* 1:1:47–54, 1969.

Wallach, M. A., and N. Kogan. *Modes of Thinking in Young Children: A Study of the Creativity-Intelligence Distinction.* New York: Holt, Rinehart, and Winston, 1965.

Wallas, G. *The Art of Thought.* London: C. A. Watts, 1926.

Warner, Sylvia Ashton. *Teacher.* New York: Simon and Schuster, 1963.

Weiner, N. *The Human Use of Human Beings: Cybernetics and Society.* London: Eyre and Spottiswoode, 1950.

Weiner, M. "The Organization of Mental Abilities for Ages 14–54." (64-2798) (Unpub. doctoral dissertation.) New York: Columbia University, 1963.

Weisberg, P. S., and K. J. Springer. "Environmental Factors in Creative Function: A Study of Gifted Children." *Archives of General Psychiatry* (Chicago), 5:554–64, 1961.

Weiss, J. "Cezanne's Technique and Scotophilia." *Psychoanalytic Quarterly,* 22:3:413–18, 1953.

Weissman, P. "Theoretical Considerations of Ego Repression and Ego Functioning in Creativity." *Psychoanalytic Quarterly*, 36:37–50, 1967.

Welsh, G. S. "Personality and Creativity: A Study of Talented High School Students." (Unpub. doctoral dissertation.) Chapel Hill: University of North Carolina, 1967.

Whelan, K. T. "A Biographical Information Blank Study of More Creative and Less Creative Occupations." (66-8037) (Unpub. doctoral dissertation.) Cleveland: Western Reserve University, 1965.

White, R. K. "A Note on the Psychopathology of Genius." *Journal of Social Psychology*, 1:311–15, 1930. (See also "Versatility of Genius." *Journal of Social Psychology*, 2:460–68, 1931.

Whiting, C. S. *Creative Thinking.* New York: Reinhold, 1958.

Williams, Frank. *Creativity at Home and School.* St. Paul: Macalester Creativity Project, Macalester College Press, 1968.

Williams, Frank. *Classroom Ideas for Encouraging Thinking and Feeling.* Buffalo, N. Y.: D. O. K. Publishing Co., 1970.

Wilson, R. C., and others. "The Measurement of Individual Differences in Originality." *Psychological Bulletin,* 50:5:262–370, Sept. 1953.

Wilson, R. N. "Poetic Creativity, Process and Personality." *Psychiatry,* 17:2:163–76, May 1954.

Winnicott, D. W. *The Maturational Processes and the Facilitating Environment: Studies in the Theory of Emotional Development.* New York: International Universities Press, 1965.

Young, M. *The Rise of Meritocracy.* London: Thames and Hudson, 1958.

Zilboorg, G. "Psychology of the Creative Personality," pp. 21–32, in *Creativity: An Examination of the Creative Process*, ed. by P. Smith. New York: Hastings House, 1959.

Author Index

Subject Index